Take My Children

Take My Children

AN ADOPTION STORY

Bernice Gottlieb

iUniverse, Inc.
Bloomington

Take My Children
An Adoption Story

Cover photo: Residents of St. Lazarus Village in Korea, 1974.

iUniverse books may be ordered through booksellers or by contacting:

iUniverse
1663 Liberty Drive
Bloomington, IN 47403
www.iuniverse.com
1-800-Authors (1-800-288-4677)

ISBN: 978-1-4502-7547-7 (sc)
ISBN: 978-1-4502-7546-0 (dj)
ISBN: 978-1-4502-7545-3 (ebk)

Library of Congress Control Number: 2010917396

Printed in the United States of America

iUniverse rev. date: 11/24/2010

For Fred

1919-2007

and for Peter, Richard and Susannah

"Bernice Gottlieb's humanitarian contribution toward helping unfortunate Korean children to lead a new life in the United States of America has established an ineradicable human bond between American and Korean people."

Korea News, Inc. New York

Table of Contents

List of Illustrations

Chapter 6 – St. Lazarus Village: Villagers waiting at the clinic to see the doctor during his monthly mobile visit.

Chapter 6 – St. Lazarus Village: Inside the clinic, where a child is being treated for burns from a rice pot.

Chapter 6 – St. Lazarus Village: Father Lee with the Chin children.

Chapter 6 – St. Lazarus Village: Some of the children at St. Lazarus Village.

Chapter 6 – St. Lazarus Village: From left: Father Lee (his broken hand in his pocket), Bernice, Raiko Kabusaki, two Carmelite nuns, a member of the St. Lazarus helpers, Young-ok, and Fred at St. Lazarus Village, March 1974.

Chapter 7 – A Difficult Search: Dr. Howard Rusk, founder of the Rusk Institute at New York University Medical Center, chairman emeritus of the American-Korean Foundation, and the "father" of rehabilitation medicine.

Chapter 8 – The Bureaucratic Nightmare: The general bill, H.R. 16737, introduced in the House by Representative Hamilton Fish, Jr., in September 1974.

Chapter 8 – The Bureaucratic Nightmare: The telegram Bernice sent to Betty Ford asking for her help.

Chapter 8 – The Bureaucratic Nightmare: Bernice and Julie Harris at a fundraiser party for Outreach: Julie had just made an eloquent speech and then introduced Bernice.

Chapter 9 – The Struggle: The general legislation introduced in the Senate by Senator Jacob Javits and recorded in the Congressional Record of January 30, 1975.

Chapter 9 – The Struggle: Marjorie Margolies and Representative Ed Mezvinsky after announcing their engagement.

Chapter 9 – The Struggle: One of the reports for the four private bills, October 1975.

Chapter 9 – The Struggle: Telegram from Bernice to Father Lee, November 18, 1975.

Chapter 10 – The Last Stretch: *The New York Times* published several supportive articles during our years of waiting.

Chapter 11 – Answered Prayers: Bernice and Father Lee with seven of the eight children the night before leaving for America.

Chapter 11 – Answered Prayers: The children dressed in their hanboks with Martha Yoon, Father Lee, and Bernice at Kimpo Airport, waiting to depart for America.

Chapter 12 – Living in the United States: The 25th reunion in 2001 at Dobbs Ferry, New York.

Afterword – At a leprosy village near Bombay, Bernice took some of the children to a shop for ice cream and sweet treats.

Afterword – Bernice was interviewed by the *Star*, Carville's in-house newspaper, in 1979.

Author's Note

In this book, I have frequently referred to Hansen's Disease as "leprosy," which is a more familiar term, even though it carries with it the heavy burden of ancient stigma. (However, I have avoided the pejorative term "leper," which unfortunately is still in use.) Many distinguished physicians and social scientists were kind enough to lead me in the right direction as I sought to learn as much as possible about this misunderstood disease before I proceeded with my plans. As a lay person, I needed to be certain that my efforts to aid the healthy children of sick parents would not pose any risk to the families so eager to adopt these children and give them a chance for a better life. The operative word here is "certain," as my responsibility weighed heavily upon me. After all, the program's success depended on convincing many people that Hansen's disease is not what myth and rumor have suggested for centuries but is a disease like any other. I knew too that the lives of thousands of children around the world could be affected by what we were planning to do. My priorities were clear and my work was cut out for me.

The names of the adoptive families have been changed to preserve their and the children's privacy.

Acknowledgments

Too many people contributed to the success of my work for me to name here, but you will find many of their names in the pages that follow and I apologize for any omissions. Three that are not mentioned are, first, Irene Kollar, my wonderful aide, who worked with me for many years. I owe her a debt of gratitude. I would also like to thank Carol Barkin, my editor and teacher, for helping me tell this story the way I wanted it told. Lastly, my dear friend Paul Gottbetter was tireless in his encouragement throughout the preparation of this book.

The most personal and steadfast support came from my grandchildren, Degen, Michael, Bobby, Samantha, Inbo, and Zoli; my children, Peter, Richard, and Susannah; my brother, Arthur Friedman; and, most of all, my incredible late husband, Fred, whom I affectionately called Ferdinando.

Bernice Gottlieb, age 6, and her brother Arthur, age 17, on a family vacation in Liberty, New York, in the Catskill Mountains.

Chapter 1. Going Home: 1934

I can remember Mrs. Thompson holding me on her lap on a fast-moving train. It was the summer of 1934, and the BMT line to Brooklyn had glassless windows with wrought-iron safety bars. It was a breezy, bumpy ride as the train went through winding tunnels, and there was a sweet, sickly subway train smell. Straddled across her lap, face to face, I remember kissing "Mama's" smiling, shiny brown face and laughing a lot. She was saying, "We're going home to your real mama, baby." I was just three years old.

In 1930, as the Depression's true weight began to be felt, my parents had suffered the tragic loss of two children in a polio epidemic. Emotionally unhinged, they were unable to take care of me when I unexpectedly came along in 1931. Mother was in the throes of a mental breakdown, and when she recovered, my father followed suit. He disappeared one day from our home in the Bronx and was found six weeks later wandering aimlessly in an amnesiac state. While he was recovering, his partners lost their nine meat supply stores and a slaughterhouse to the faltering economy. My parents had to start all over again.

Eventually my father's cousin gave him a job at his small butcher shop in Brooklyn. Mother and Dad left their home in the Bronx in the spring of 1934 when Dad found an apartment in Brooklyn near the shop. It consisted of three small rooms in a pretentious-looking building with a doorman. The lobby had Tennessee marble floors and walls, an ornate fireplace, and gilded maroon velvet benches. Our apartment was on the lobby floor at the back of the building overlooking the courtyard and back alley. Our rent was $42.50 a month. This is where I grew up.

Mother had not known she was pregnant when my brother Robert and sister Dorothy took ill and died just weeks apart. When I was born, she gave my care over to her friend Mrs. Thompson, who had given birth to her own child a few months earlier. My surviving brother Arthur, who was eleven years old when I was born, came with me.

Mrs. Thompson and her husband lived in Harlem, and Mother knew her from their days in silent films. Mrs. Thompson had been a wardrobe mistress at the old Biograph Studios in the Bronx where Mother was a bit player and where my brother Arthur had made nine movies with Milton Sills; Sills was a popular and prolific actor, a heartthrob in the twenties. Arthur and I lived with the Thompsons off and on for more than three years, visiting our parents regularly while they were getting their lives back together again. After returning home, it took me quite a while to think of myself as a white person.

During one overnight visit home when Mother was feeling stronger, I ran a high fever and went into convulsions. This was enough to set her back again. She felt she didn't have the capacity to keep her children alive. There is an ancient Hebrew ceremony to quell such fears, and so Mother consulted with a rabbi and asked for this rite to be performed. A family with healthy children volunteered to participate and to "adopt" me. My Hebrew name was changed at this ceremony in order to fool the Angel of Death.

When I was about eight, I came home from school one day to find Mother crying. It was winter and she sat in a kitchen chair near the radiator. Our Friday night Shabbat dinner was cooking on the stove behind her. She was wearing an apron; she blotted her eyes when I came in.

"Mommy, what's the matter?" I asked, saddened by her red-rimmed eyes.

"Sorry, love, but I have the wigwams," Mother said. I had heard her use that expression before. I knew it meant she was depressed. I put my school case down, took off my galoshes and overcoat, and put my arms around her. She gathered me close to her soft large bosom, and the scent of rosewater and glycerin filled my nostrils.

Then she told me about Dorothy and Robert for the first time. I was terribly upset to know I could have had a sister and another brother.

"It was a polio epidemic," she said, rocking me in her arms. "Daddy wanted us to go to South Fallsburg for vacation even though he knew there was talk of an epidemic. We never should have gone."

Then she said something that has haunted me. "When I was giving birth to you, I had a dream. I dreamed that Dorothy was smiling at me and saying, 'Don't worry, Mommy, I'm coming back,' and then my lovely baby girl was born. I was so happy you were a girl."

Her words made me wonder whether I was Dorothy or me. I didn't really understand what she was saying. Dorothy and Robert were never again discussed in my presence, but every Friday night Mother lit candles for them. And I remembered an incident from when I was four or five years old. My mother and father were sitting at the tall secretary desk in our living room. Photograph albums were kept in its bottom drawer, and they were looking at one of them. Mother was crying, and my father had his arm around her shoulders.

I could see that they were looking at pictures of a little boy and a little girl I had never seen. That night I had a dream (which recurred for a long time) of two little white caskets being carried down the long entry hall of our apartment. Mother was walking behind them, and she was screaming. Soon after that, I took my box of crayons and scribbled on all the photographs of the little boy and girl, blotting out their faces completely.

Chapter 2. The Gift of Young-ah: 1968

I had never thought about *adopting* a child. We had discussed having a third child, but Fred was pushing fifty and wasn't into the baby/ not sleeping/diaper mode. In 1967, my good friend Shirley Collins had a miscarriage and was told she should not try again to become pregnant. I was visiting her right after the miscarriage, and she was distraught. I suggested she try to adopt a child, and I said she should find out whether Vietnamese children were being brought into the country. (The war was still raging, and pictures of napalm-bombed children were in everyone's psyches.) Caucasian babies were almost impossible to get, and in any case, Shirley was borderline in terms of age and probably would not qualify through the usual channels. Shirley was intimidated by my suggestion and asked me to make inquiries on her behalf. I agreed, but I soon learned that the Vietnamese were not sending many children out of the country as they did not have a social welfare system in place because of the war. I had to find another way to help my friend.

By coincidence, around this time there was an article in *The New York Times Magazine* about thousands of children languishing in Korean orphanages. It stressed the fact that adoption in Korea was not a socially acceptable concept, and so these children would remain in the orphanages until they were mature enough to live on their own.

I contacted a number of people involved with Korea, including their consulate and the Korean Desk at the State Department. After much research and accumulation of bureaucratic forms and applications, I presented this information to Shirley and her husband, Bob. But, after all was said and done, they just didn't have the courage to adopt a child of another race and culture. In fact, they never adopted at all. But that's how Fred and I ended up adopting a child from South Korea. We were already blessed with two wonderful sons and hoped we could find a daughter to complete our family.

Our first step was to obtain a home study from an accredited government agency. The nearest social service agency was in White Plains, New York, so we made an appointment with a social worker. It was a really exciting thought: a child from another culture who needed a home. Why, after all, should we bring another child into this world when so many children needed a loving family?

After several hours of questions during two meetings, the social worker turned us down as prospective adoptive parents. She simply could not comprehend a) why we didn't simply have another biological child and b) why we wanted an Asian child and not an American baby. To her, we were suspect.

But we were shocked, and I went on the warpath. We made an appointment with the Commissioner of Social Services, Louis Kurtis. After discussing our situation, he was in total agreement that we should be approved as prospective adoptive parents. The problem was, though, that as a local social service agency they could do a home study for us (a requirement for adoption), but they had never reached out to children outside the United States. He said they had no contacts with a cooperating child placement service in

Korea or, for that matter, with an agency in New York State that worked overseas. I told him I was willing to do some research and find the contacts he needed. We were quickly approved and I went right to work.

Adopting from abroad was still a relatively new concept, but I found an agency that did some adoption work—International Social Service (later Traveler's Aid—International Social Service of America, or TAISSA) and we worked with them. I felt wonderful; it was like being pregnant. TAISSA was in touch with a Korean adoption service, Social Welfare Society, in Seoul and sent us a photograph of a six-year-old girl named Jin Sook. Fred and I felt that because this was such an important decision, we should see the child before agreeing to adopt her. We planned a trip to Korea that would also include a family wedding in Australia. However, a few days before we were to depart, Fred's mother died, and so I went alone, to Korea only.

Fred was sophisticated, artistic, and very romantic. He and his family had escaped from Germany in 1934 when Fred was a teenager, and I admired the fact that he had emigrated to the United States alone when he was just seventeen. He made his way courageously and eventually enlisted in the army in 1940, a year before Pearl Harbor. He became a company commander in army intelligence and won two bronze stars for successful operations on Omaha Beach in Normandy. After five years with the 9th Army Air Force, he enrolled at Columbia University's School of Architecture and, after eight years there, became an architect. He had come from a privileged background in Berlin that was all lost to him when Hitler came to power, but he showed his determination in a new country and on his own. Best of all, he believed in me, and because he did, I felt there was nothing I couldn't accomplish. Literally, he was the wind beneath my wings.

As I sat on the plane, I thought about how quickly we had reached the decision to adopt. And then the many months of frustration, explanations, and paperwork that had followed. Even the decision to go to Korea and select a child ourselves had been fraught with difficulty. It was not normally done, the agency had said. But they had come to understand that because of our many Korean friends and our firm determination to meet the child we planned to bring into our family, this was not negotiable.

Our friend Ja Kyung Koo had written to her parents, Mr. and Mrs. Koo, in Seoul about our search. Already they had located a child for our consideration. They had even sent a contingent of elderly family members to the orphanage to examine the child Korean-style. This meant looking at the shape of her eyes to determine her character and if she was wise, and her ears to see if she would have a long life. They had found everything satisfactory and were anxious for me to see her.

The plane took the northwest route to Japan, flying over Anchorage, Alaska. I was so elated that every sight along the way took on special meaning. It was too bad Fred couldn't share all of this with me, I thought, but his mother's death had left him with much to take care of.

After many hours we approached the coast of Japan and the plane went into its descent. Lovely wooden and rice paper structures dotted the landscape. The harbor was filled with Japanese naval vessels as far as the eye could see. I changed planes in Tokyo for the trip over the Sea of Japan to Korea. A young soldier from the Midwest took the seat next to me, pleased to find an American woman aboard.

"Why are you traveling to that godforsaken place?" he asked, incredulous. I somewhat reluctantly told him about our plan to adopt a Korean child.

"Well, I've just returned from R&R in Japan," he confided. "Thank God, I've only got four months left to go in Korea!"

As we talked, I realized that he was a very bitter, homesick young man. One reason for his despair was that his close friend had died in a border skirmish on the DMZ.

We were preparing to land, so I busied myself collecting my belongings. I remembered the name tag written in phonetic Korean that Ja Kyung Koo had made for me and pinned it on.

The terminal at Kimpo Airport was small and very hot, the customs agent bureaucratic, but I finally made it through. A handsome young man dressed elegantly in white rushed forward to meet me. It was Ja Ik Koo, our friend's brother. He welcomed me in halting English, bowing formally from the waist. Then, taking my luggage, he led me to his waiting car.

On the way to the hotel we drove through the darkening city. Everything in my view looked beautiful and so different. Women in their traditional long dresses carried babies strapped to their backs. Oxen perambulated the unpaved streets amidst skyscrapers, and bicycles loaded high and wide with merchandise made their way aggressively through the congested traffic.

After seeing me to my room at the hotel, Ja Ik explained that he and his sister would pick me up first thing in the morning. They had arranged appointments at several orphanages, he said, including the Orphans' Home of Korea where the child his parents had chosen for us lived. They would take me to these orphanages after my first appointment at Social Welfare Society, which had been arranged by TAISSA.

Alone at last, I threw my shoes off and collapsed into a chair. I looked at my watch. It was exactly twenty-three hours since I had left New York—no wonder I was so tired. The room was hot and humid, the air conditioner ineffective. But after all, I reflected, August in Korea was not exactly April in Paris. I opened the window, hoping for some fresh air. An unimpeded view of the Han River and bridge greeted me. Chinese-style junks were slowly maneuvering through the night, illuminated by the moon. I stood transfixed. It was breathtakingly beautiful, more like a dream than reality.

The next morning the Koos' limousine took me to Social Welfare Society and I met its director, Youn Taek Tahk. I sat in his office, surrounded by several social workers, and Jin Sook was brought in from the countryside to meet me. She had been abandoned as an infant and had never had a family. Now she had been told she was going to be adopted.

At age six she was bent over from rickets and pathetically thin. I had brought many gifts with me, and I felt so sorry for her that I gave her all of them. My heart was breaking; after two hours with her, I knew she was not the right choice for us. All these years later, I still think about her, how hopeful she was, and how I disappointed that poor child.

After I left Social Welfare Society, the limousine made its way through crowded streets, heading away from the city. The road worsened as we approached the Seoul suburbs, the car taking the bumps with squeaks and groans. Ja Ik sat in front with the driver. His sister Ja Yung, her friend Sung Wha Oh, and I were together in the backseat of the car, which was furnished with embroidered satin cushions. The two women, educated in the United States, were fluent in English and very chic, charming company.

Ja Yung told me that Mrs. On Soon Whang, the director of the Orphans' Home of Korea, had already become a legendary figure in her country. The property on which the orphanage was built had belonged to her son, who had been killed in action during the Korean War. Mrs. Whang had cared for thousands of orphans since then, in honor of her son, and she hoped someday to build a school for underprivileged girls on the site.

"She has never placed any of her children in adoption before," Ja Yung told me. "This time she is willing to do so because of her friendship with my parents."

"The child she has found is eighteen months old," Sung Wha added. "Her name is Chung Young-ah. You know, we put our family name first in Korea," she informed me. [Note: I have used "American style" (surname last) for the Korean names in this book, because most of the sources I have quoted from use this style.] Young-ah was a "special" child from a prominent family who had lived for her first year with her mother—secretly, as her mother was not married—and was then placed with Mrs. Whang.

We entered the grounds of the orphanage and I couldn't disguise my excitement. I could see some of the older children working in the rice fields, knee-deep in water. Stopping in front of a stuccoed cottage, we took our shoes off and went inside. An elderly servant showed us into a study, then left the room backwards, still bowing. We waited for Mrs. Whang to learn of our arrival.

She swept into the room almost immediately, her beauty and energy belying her seventy-odd years. After the introduction, we sat on floor mats around a low tea table, chatting. The elderly servant reappeared with a tray of tall glasses filled with Coca-Cola. It was another scorchingly hot day, and I was bathed in perspiration. The women used gossamer sheets of rice paper to blot the moisture on their faces. They offered me a packet, which I gratefully accepted.

I sat patiently for a long time while they continued to converse, mainly in Korean. Finally, there was a knock at the door. A nurse appeared, carrying a tiny, moon-faced child, beautifully dressed in yellow silk.

"So here is Young-ah," Mrs. Whang said proudly. She held her arms out to the child and Young-ah responded, smiling familiarly at Mrs. Whang. However, the child noticed me after a moment and blanched. Hiding her face behind her hands, she peeked out between her fingers and started to cry.

"Please do not worry," Mrs. Whang said reassuringly to me. "She has never before seen a European woman. Perhaps your eyes look strange to her. Anyway, she will soon be calm."

The nurse quickly removed Young-ah from the room, comforting her with soft words. Once outside, the child's crying abated. When all was quiet, Mrs. Whang suggested I go into the next room. I did so at once, opening the door slowly. Young-ah sat alone on the floor, a bowl of grapes at her side. She was meticulously peeling each grape and neatly disposing of the skins and pits. I sat down near her. She seemed less intimidated but retained some suspicion. Then her eyes fixed on the drink in my hand. She asked, without shyness, "Young-ah, Coca-cola?"

I pointed to my lap, hoping she would want the drink badly enough to come closer. As everyone watched through a crack in the study door, Young-ah came to me, both hands reaching for the soda glass. As she drank, I saw that she had long, beautiful fingers.

"Kam sa," she said politely, returning to her grapes.

I was suddenly struck by the overwhelming size of the task at hand. There were thousands of children out there, just like this little one. I was in a position to choose any one of them. Despite the heat, a chill ran through my body. How would I make such a choice? What if there was something wrong with the child? Was I doing the right thing? Young-ah toddled over again, had a little more Coke, then unexpectedly curled up in my lap and began to fall asleep. This stirred up all kinds of emotions. Mrs. Whang came out of the study, nodding her head in approval. The full realization of what I was doing continued to absorb me. This was not as easy a decision as I had thought.

"Young-ah is a lovely child, Mrs. Whang," I said, softly so as not to disturb her sleep, "but she is a bit young for our family. I hope you won't mind if I see other children before I make such an important decision."

"Young-ah is a special child," Mrs. Whang agreed, "but you are right. Let me show you some of my other children and then you must visit many orphanages. When you find the right child, you will know it," she said, her eyes full of wisdom.

As I cradled the sleeping toddler, three other children were brought into the room. The same nurse who had carried Young-ah now guided them toward me. They were between four and five years old. Pretty little girls, they were holding hands as they shyly approached. On closer inspection, I saw that the first child was covered almost entirely with warts, the second had blond hair and pigmented patches on her face, arms and legs, and the last child wore leg braces. My heart went out to all of them. I knew Mrs. Whang was trying to tell me something.

That afternoon and the days that followed were a blur of activity. We spent the time drinking ginseng tea and visiting orphanages, touring the museums and historical sites and visiting orphanages, even getting me fitted for a traditional Korean hanbok and visiting more orphanages. We were a relentless gang of four until Ja Yung, Ja Ik, and I were finally too exhausted to continue. I had already compiled a longer list of eligible children than was necessary. After all, all I needed was one little girl.

After each day of searching, I went back to see Young-ah again. Young-ah was not beautiful (yet!), and I had promised Fred that I would choose an older child, close to school age. But there was something about her that drew me back. None of the other children I had met reached me the same way.

"Just one more orphanage," Sung Wha pleaded. "This is too important to allow laziness to get in the way!" This last remark shamed me into agreeing. But Ja Yung and Ja Ik looked relieved when I said it wasn't necessary for them to join us.

"Okay, Sung Wha," I declared, giving in to her unflagging energy and spirit. "But then, my friend, let's call it quits!"

We drove to a small inlet. Sung Wha instructed the driver to wait there for us. We walked along a floating pier, then climbed into an antiquated boat with two other passengers. They were elderly men, with wispy beards, stovepipe hats, and harem pants. They looked charming. Curious, they asked Sung Wha the reason for my Korean visit. When she explained, they smiled and nodded their heads appreciatively, one of the old men patting my arm to show his approval. When we reached the other side of the river, Sung Wha and I walked uphill in the hot sun for a while before reaching our destination. Upon our arrival, we were very disappointed to learn that the orphanage was only for boys. We had made the trip for nothing. At this point, however, we were both philosophical. Parched, we gratefully accepted the offer of iced tea from the orphanage director. It was made with tap water, and later we regretted our carelessness when both of us became terribly ill.

In my hotel room that night, between bouts of nausea and vomiting, I wallowed in self-pity and doubt. I had seen too many children, many of them sick or malnourished--a sea of anonymity, it seemed. I cried and cried. How could I ever pick only one of them? It seemed impossible. What was I doing here on the other side of the world, anyway? What a dumb idea this had been. Oh, how I wished Fred were here with me. Finally, close to dawn, I fell asleep.

In the morning I woke with a clear head. All signs of my physical distress had gone. Somehow in the morass of the night, everything had clarified. I knew exactly what I was going to do. I would choose Young-ah, of course. I had wanted her from the very beginning. I just hadn't realized it was possible to make such an important decision so quickly and I hadn't wanted to be influenced by the Koo family's well-meaning preference. But I should have known better. After all, Fred and I had recognized our special feelings for one another immediately, marrying just ten weeks after we met. Young-ah had affected me the same way.

The night, the nausea, the doubt, even the bout of self-pity had all served their purpose. I telephoned New York to tell Fred the good news. The timing was just right and I not only reached him but spoke as well to my dear little boys.. We agreed over the telephone to rename Young-ah. We would call her Susannah, Fred's favorite girl's name—one he identified as "real Americana."

When I told Mrs. Whang I had come to a decision, she was very pleased. "Forgive me for saying this," she said, "but because I am a Buddhist, I believe the decision was actually not yours to make. It was decided millions of years ago."

There is much to be said for the wisdom of the Orient.

Before leaving Korea, I said my goodbyes to all the wonderful people who had helped me in Seoul, and especially to Mr. Koo, who had been such a generous host. It was August 15 when I made the decision to adopt Young-ah, and he made a speech in front of his family. He talked about the occupation by Japan and said that my decision had been made on a special day—Independence Day from Japan. Then he congratulated me on taking a child from his beloved country to give her a loving home in America. It was very touching, and I will never forget this charming, handsome man.

Back in the United States, I got to work filling out all the necessary papers. TAISSA was upset that I had not taken the child they had found for me, but I was content in the knowledge that Young-ah would be a better fit for Peter and Richard. In 1968 foreign adoption was rare in the New York metropolitan area, and neighbors had heard about our adoption plans. The local media picked up the story and I was photographed wearing a Korean hanbok, with my sons. Even before Susannah (as we started calling her) arrived, I received calls from other families who wanted to do the same thing. Westchester County had recently geared up to help families with international adoptions, and because we were the first to do it, prospective couples were sent to us to get answers to procedural questions. Some people in government still found it strange that anyone wanted to adopt a child from another culture; I told them such children were simply flowers from another garden.

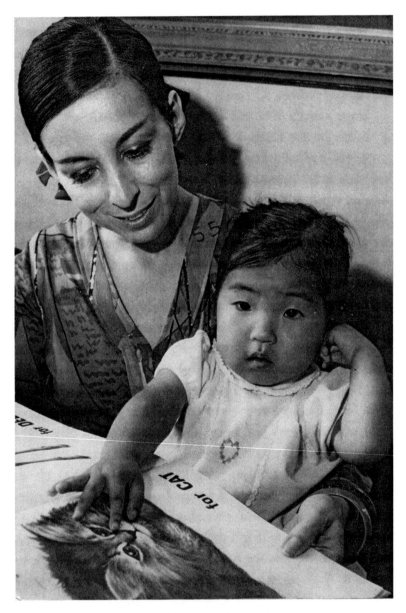

Bernice with Susannah (age three).

Once Susannah arrived, on June 4, 1969, we were constantly stopped—on the street, in restaurants—and asked if she was adopted. I ended up inviting perfect strangers to our home on Friday nights after dinner. At first there were two or three couples, but after a while there were dozens of families. I think the surge of interest was because of the television footage we were all watching about Vietnam and the children being injured or orphaned. Our consciences were stirred by their terrible suffering.

This was happening all across the country. I began connecting with other grassroots organizations, and before long I had lists of prospective adoptive parents from New York to the state of Washington. At one point I was given a grant from the Edna McConnell Clark Foundation to coordinate under one umbrella some 30,000 families who were interested in transracial adoption, which was almost entirely from Asia at the time. I called it the Committee of 1000, which was an existing group in the Midwest led by Clayton Hagen. Clayton worked with me and a few others, such as Kathy Sreedhar of Washington, D.C., John Adams of the Holt Agency in Oregon, and Gerald Adcock, a lobbyist for the Ford Motor Company in Washington. We were early pioneers of international adoption in the United States and worked together for many years.

The families kept coming every Friday night—huge numbers of people in the house wanting to know how they could adopt. They wanted advice and they thought I was the source of information about foreign adoption. Some were from important or well-known families, but most were middle-class or lower middle-class; I found that this group had the most interest in adoption, wanting to share what they had with someone less fortunate.

I had of course been in touch with Westchester County's Department of Social Services, which oversaw everything having to do with adoptions. The Commissioner, Louis Kurtis, gave me a letter in October 1972 that said his department would "cooperate in the adoption placement and supervision in Westchester County of children of Korean or Chinese ancestry referred through appropriate channels...under the auspices of Mrs. Bernice Gottlieb." This was because of the work I had been doing with families interested in transracial adoptions, but it turned out to be a very important support for my later work.

Chapter 3. Outreach Is Born: 1972

As I continued volunteering on behalf of children, I started finding homes for handicapped children as well. In Korea, because of my relationship with Youn Taek Tahk of Social Welfare Society, word got out that Americans were adopting children with disabilities. And in the Korean community in Westchester it was also known. My friend Clara Han called me one summer day in 1972 and invited me to her home in Yonkers to meet Father Alexander Lee from Korea, who was a childhood friend of hers. She said he had some children he wished to send to America. I was surprised to learn that he was the administrator of a leprosy resettlement community (a polite term for a leprosy colony) in Suwon, Anyang Province, about fifteen miles south of Seoul.

Father Lee was a slight man who spoke excellent English. He described the horrible treatment that the healthy children of parents with leprosy had to endure. They could not go to public schools and were required to carry special identification cards. He said that leprosy is a misunderstood disease and the Korean culture had many superstitions about the victims of leprosy, including the belief that people with leprosy kidnapped small children to eat their livers as a cure. The children of those with leprosy are called "mundungi," or leper's whelp, and "mikama," which means not yet infected.

"The stigma is worse than the disease itself," Father Lee said. "There are drugs today that are available to anyone with leprosy and they are inexpensive and effective. Also, the disease is not very contagious, nor is it hereditary." He paused. "What the children do inherit is society's fear, and that is the problem."

Father Lee then showed me eight photographs of smiling children ranging in age from infancy to twelve. He said that he had tried to get these children into several countries but had been turned down by their immigration authorities. Furthermore, none of their relatives on the "outside" would take them nor would other, more educated and enlightened Koreans. His voice full of emotion, he said, "I want very much for you to find homes for these children in America."

"But if these children have parents, how can they be willing to give them up? Don't they love them?" I asked.

"Well, you see, it's precisely because of their love that they are willing to make such a sacrifice. There's nothing for them to look forward to if they stay where they are. You sometimes have to be cruel to be kind." He explained that their parents wanted these children to have a life free of stigma—to have a proper education and to leave the confines of their restricted colony.

Then Father Lee told me this story about Mr. Cho.

Te Chong Cho looked sadly at his wife. "No one will take the children. I have even talked to my father's cousin in Chun Nam Province. The truth is that no one wants to have mikama in their house. They will just have to stay with us."

Hee Kyung was asleep, her tiny body strapped securely to her mother's back, and little Mee Kyung, her older sister, played contentedly with some colored beads on the bare floor, oblivious to her parents' distress.

The Cho family lived in a small room in one of the dormitories at St. Lazarus Village, sharing a communal kitchen with two other families. It was a bitter cold winter, and Te Chong Cho counted his twentieth year at the village, having arrived during the winter of 1952. Mr. Cho was thirty-three years old and could no longer remember what life had been like in his old village. His wife had been abandoned to St. Lazarus when she was seventeen because of a skin problem on her legs that resembled leprosy. By the time it was diagnosed as eczema, she had fallen in love with Te Chong Cho and decided to marry him and remain at the village.

Mr. Cho's hands were severely deformed due to late diagnosis of his illness. He had been told recently that gangrene was now threatening his right leg and that he would eventually need amputation in order to survive. His depression deepened with each day as he worried about the future of his beloved daughters, who were healthy and beautiful. He prayed that they would have an opportunity to leave St. Lazarus so they could have a better life and an education, which he knew he could never provide. But he believed this to be an impossible dream.

Father Lee ended his story, and the two of us looked at each other in silence. I was uncomfortable with the idea of separating parents and children; orphans and abandoned children had always been my priority. But as Father Lee continued talking, I began to understand more clearly. If these children could pass immigration inspection in the United States, that would be a strong statement to the Korean people. Our accepting them in spite of our very restrictive immigration policies would prove that these children were healthy and would not be a danger to others. The Korean people would be impressed by this and would perhaps begin to look more favorably at granting these victims of society's prejudice their basic human rights. This might eventually mean that thousands of such children could be integrated into the public schools in Korea.

As we spoke, Father Lee coughed a lot; he said he had just recovered from tuberculosis and had serious heart disease. He didn't know how long he could take care of the four hundred families at St. Lazarus Village.

I knew nothing about leprosy then, or Hansen's disease as it is properly known (named for Dr. Gerhard A. Hansen who first described the bacteria that causes it in 1894). But as I listened to Father Lee speak, I already knew this was something I was going to do. He told me about the many villages like his own and what a pitiful state the children were in. He spoke, close to tears, about the difficulty of managing without so much as one resident doctor and about the pressing needs for food, clothing, and shelter. Mainly, he repeated the problems confronting the stigmatized, healthy children.

We shook hands on a promise that I would find out if there was any hope of taking even a few of these children into the United States as a symbol of their dilemma. But as our conversation continued, Father Lee told me that some children from leprosy villages had quietly reached the States through traditional orphanage channels, their true origins kept from both the orphanage and the adoptive parents. I told Father Lee that I would want my efforts to stand for more than such a meek, camouflaged, and limited activity; it would be a do-or-die campaign to bring into the open the devastating plight of these children throughout the world and to effect their legal, willing adoption in this country. After all, all the children living in segregated leprosy villages would benefit from such an effort.

I thought of these children as normal in every respect, except that they were pariahs in their country. In every case, their parents' leprosy was arrested and had been even before the children were born. Still, the children were feared and hated by society, forced to live apart from the community and to endure the pejorative terms of mundungi and mikama. I wanted to play a small part in alerting the world to this injustice and to improve the quality of life for all healthy children living in such enforced segregation. Since America has the toughest health requirements in the world, bringing even a few of the children here would send a strong message to those societies who are fearful of this disease and ruin so many lives because of their ignorance.

I told Father Lee that I would try to learn whether our laws would permit the entry of such children. Then I added impetuously, "I tell you what. If they do, I'll help you."

He took both my hands into his own and said exultantly, "Thank God!"

As Father Lee said goodbye, I realized that I was taking on more than an army of do-gooders had been able to accomplish for decades. Who was I, with literally no knowledge of the disease or of the monumental legal process, to attempt such an undertaking? The question would be asked so many times: why was I doing this? I could only say that I felt as though I had been preprogrammed to do it.

On my way home, I couldn't help thinking about my own difficult beginning: Mother, sick with a nervous breakdown after the deaths of my sister Dorothy and brother Robert, and Dad, losing all he'd worked for during those terrible years of the Depression and also succumbing to their terrible loss. I was stirred deeply by the plight of the children Father Lee had spoken about. Sick parents, a difficult life situation, grim poverty, and shocking prejudice. No wonder these loving parents considered sending their children out of Korea.

I didn't sleep well that night, and I remembered Mrs. Thompson. I had cried for her for months after she returned me to my parents.

The only one who could comfort me was Arthur. He was always there for me. He had made a beaded ring for me, and I used to sleep with it every night. I thought too about my dear children. Could I make such a sacrifice, sending them away if their lives were miserable? There were so many parallels to my own life.

The next day I started making calls to find out what our laws said about the entry of the Korean children into the United States. My first concern was the health issue. I called a distant cousin in Washington, D.C., Dr. Jesse Steinfeld, who was then Surgeon General of the United States, but he was in Europe and would not be back for two weeks. I told his secretary why I was calling, and she suggested that I call the Center for Disease Control in Atlanta.

I spoke to Dr. Robert Giordano, acting director of the Foreign Quarantine Program of the CDC, about the children's situation, and he said he would get back to me after researching the immigration restrictions on health issues. The following day he called to tell me that there were no restrictions on healthy children who had been exposed to leprosy. I asked Dr. Giordano to give me a letter to that effect; on October 18, 1972, he wrote me that "There are no regulations in the Public Health Service or elsewhere, as far as I know, which restrict the entry into this country of children who have parents or relatives who have leprosy. I do not believe that any state regulations would restrict the entry of such children into the state." This was very good news.

I kept in touch with Father Lee, and in October 1972 I received a letter from him. He wrote in part, "While I was traveling in the States and Europe, I received various impressions and many things are regarded to be Providence of God. Especially the unexpected meeting with you was designed by His Will to show what we should do for these unfortunate children. You are a person of much potentiality, who know many people, who received proper education, and who have confidence in self. It is my great pleasure that I could see the person who has the same interest and is working actually for it. When we cooperate with each other, how much help and happiness we will be able to give to them!" His words reinforced my determination to find a way to bring the children to America.

I had assumed that these children would qualify for entry in the same way orphans and abandoned children did, but I soon learned that children with parents generally had to come in under the quota system. However, the quota for Asia was backed up for years; I would have to find another way to get them here quickly. I naively thought that this was not a huge challenge, that the government would look kindly on the plight of these children once I brought their desperate situation to the attention of the right people.

I am painfully aware that naiveté is a large component of my personal makeup. Yet I am also grateful, as otherwise I might not have attempted to be the catalyst for such an unusual breaking of shibboleths.

I started to put a lot of wheels into motion. Earlier, through my work finding homes for Korean children, I had met Marjorie Margolies. She had been given my name as a person who could find homes for hard-to-place children. Margie was a reporter for NBC News and a single adoptive parent of two daughters, Lee Heh from Korea and Holly from Vietnam. Lee Heh had left two brothers behind when she emigrated. She had been cautioned by the Korean social worker who handled her adoption not to mention her brothers, as it might interfere with her own emigration; however, she eventually told Margie about them (they were now teenagers) and asked Margie to help bring them into the States. I offered my assistance and found homes for the boys; as this was going on, Margie and I became friends.

I talked to Margie now, and she introduced me to her friend Nancy Chasen, who was a personal assistant to Ralph Nader. Nancy felt that I was going to have difficulty overcoming the immigration guidelines, and she spent time explaining how Washington operated with regard to making such challenges work.

Around the same time, I started my search for an American adoption agency that would sponsor these children. For international adoptions, an agency like TAISSA (Traveler's Aid International Social Service Agency) was necessary. They had connections with overseas agencies, and they could coordinate the home studies of prospective adoptive parents and help facilitate the approvals without which children could not enter this country. In fact, the federal government would not support the children's emigration without the involvement of a registered child placement agency. (My search for such an agency, which lasted about two years, unexpectedly would become a nightmare.)

I talked to people at TAISSA first, around November 1972, because they had worked with me on Susannah's adoption; they agreed to work with me on Father Lee's project. I also began putting out feelers to prospective adoptive parents for this unusual program. The usual rules of adoption had to be put aside. Father Lee initially insisted on Catholic parents, but I quickly put that notion to rest. Looking him square in the eye, I said that the parents had to be very special to take an older child, a child from a leprosy background, and one who would be in touch with the biological parents from day one. I pointed out that the adoptive parents had to be comfortable with the fact that this adopted child would have the choice to return home to Korea at will. Not too many families would be so unselfish. I also told him that I needed to get permission from the Korean and American governments to accept qualified single parents as well. Father Lee didn't mention the religious backgrounds of the parents after that. As it eventually turned out, two of the adoptive families were Catholic and the other two were Protestant but willing to give the children a Catholic upbringing if necessary.

It was clear that this project was going to take up a lot of time and energy, but luckily I didn't have to do all of it myself. There were a number of people who had been working with me on and off on adoptions of Korean children and then of "hard-to place" children from overseas. All of them cared deeply about the fate of orphans and other children in need. Their hard work and generosity were essential components in making our project happen.

Chapter 4. Carville, Louisiana: 1973

After the CDC's assurance that there were no restrictions that would prevent the entry of healthy children of parents who had leprosy, I started researching the options for their emigration to America. I also wanted to learn about the disease, as I needed to feel certain myself that there would not be any health risk. Arthur, teasing me, said that either I would be a hero if this program worked or I would be responsible for a major leprosy epidemic if it didn't.

It was now 1973, and I met Dr. Bruce Grynbaum, a doctor of rehabilitation medicine, at the Rusk Institute at New York University Medical Center, while I was in the hospital with a back problem. I asked him if he knew of any institution that taught tropical diseases, specifically leprosy, to non-physicians. He explained that most American doctors had read one paragraph in their medical textbooks about Hansen's disease, but then he remembered seeing an advertisement in one of the medical journals about a course at the U.S. Public Health Service Hospital in Carville, Louisiana— the only leprosarium in the continental United States. He located the journal the following day and I saw that this was an intensive eight-day course given by American Leprosy Missions, a Baptist organization that supported Christian missionary work to combat leprosy in many countries. Only forty-five qualified persons would be accepted for the course. I called the organization from my hospital bed the next day and was given an appointment for two weeks later to meet with Dr. Oliver Hasselblad, president of the group and an expert on leprosy. I hoped to be out of the hospital in time.

Dr. Hasselblad leaned back in his chair, his arms folded on his chest. His thinning red hair was accented by sunlight streaming in through the narrow window behind him. "I am sorry, Mrs. Gottlieb," he said, "but I must tell you I am completely at odds with what you are trying to do. I hope you will change your plans."

I was shocked. I had made the appointment to see him with so much enthusiasm. The room was paneled in dark wood. Several religious articles including a large wooden cross adorned the walls, giving the room the appearance of a church office. I felt my Jewish insecurity surfacing. Was the doctor's negative attitude influenced by our religious differences, I wondered?

"Dr. Hasselblad," I said, "yours is the only leprosy course I know of and I am really interested in learning more about the disease. I hope you will give me the opportunity to do so regardless of how I use the information."

He frowned, then leaned forward, placing his elbows on the desk. "The problem is," he said, "we can only accept a limited number of participants. We have received many requests already from doctors, nurses, and religious workers. Just how committed to all of this are you? Committed enough to take a seat away from one of these dedicated people?"

I was annoyed at the way he phrased his question. Of course I was committed. Otherwise I wouldn't be sitting in his office. "Would you be good enough to tell me why you are against bringing these children here?" I asked. "I would think that you, of all people, would be supportive of such efforts."

He got up from his chair and went to a nearby metal cabinet. From under a pile of medical journals he pulled out a book, dropping it noisily on the desk in front of me. "Here, read this when you get home," he said. "It is about institutions known as preventoria. Children used to be forcibly taken from their sick parents and isolated in these places. It was believed they would benefit healthwise from the separation. Instead, however, most of them died from starvation."

I wondered how he could equate such horrible practices with what I intended doing. In our case, it was the parents themselves who had initiated the action. They had begged Father Lee to get their children out of the colony and into adoptive homes overseas. They wanted a better life for them, free of stigma.

I sat facing Dr. Hasselblad, not knowing what else to say. I had already explained all of this to him. However, he apparently had a closed mind on the subject. I gathered the papers I had shared with him and prepared to leave. He watched me in silence for a few moments and then said, "Have you ever seen anyone with leprosy, Mrs. Gottlieb? Aren't you afraid you might find the experience rather disturbing?"

"Look, Dr. Hasselblad, I spent many years as a volunteer at various institutions for the handicapped. Many of the people I worked with had congenital deformities so horrible that they rarely ventured out in public. I am sure, from all I have read, that leprosy is nowhere near as disfiguring."

His expression didn't change at all at this revelation. I almost thought he hadn't heard me, but then he spoke again. "That may be so, but what about the would-be adoptive parents? They don't have your experience. Take my word for it, the minute one of these kids comes down with a simple skin rash or a case of ringworm, these families will panic. That is not a healthy psychological atmosphere for children." I started to speak but he interrupted me. "In my opinion," he continued, "they will run into as much fear and ignorance here as they encounter in South Korea. Besides, I firmly believe that children should never be removed from their own culture regardless of their life situation."

We were certainly poles apart. I wondered what he would have thought had he known about Susannah or my involvement in international adoption. But there was no point in going into any of this. When we said goodbye, we weren't any closer in understanding than when we had started.

"Let me give you a piece of advice," he said, walking me out to the elevator in the hall. "Don't get involved in something you know nothing about. You may unwittingly do more harm than good." He paused a moment, waiting for my response to his warning. When I said nothing, he continued, a bit more kindly. "If you should decide to go ahead with your plans, then do so with your head and not your heart."

I did not expect to hear from Dr. Hasselblad again after our meeting. It was too bad, I thought. I had really hoped for his blessing. However, I did not believe he was entirely correct about moving the children. I had some reservations of my own about the parent-child separation and had discussed this matter at length with a number of social workers and child psychiatrists. That was one reason I wanted to attend the leprosy course. I felt I would be better able to understand the effects of adoption on the children if I understood more about the social aspects of the disease.

Within a few days, a letter arrived from Dr. Hasselblad's organization, American Leprosy Missions. I held my breath as I opened it. To my astonishment, my application for the seminar had been approved; I would be one of the forty-five participants. I was grateful to the doctor, knowing he would have preferred to turn me down but hadn't done so. Perhaps he had some doubts after our meeting, or maybe he felt the course would convince me to give up my controversial idea. Whatever the reason, I looked forward to going to Louisiana the following month.

An entry from my Carville diary: April 25, 1973

I'm en route to Atlanta, there to catch a connecting flight to New Orleans and from there a bus to Carville, Louisiana, on the banks of the Mississippi River, seventy miles northwest of New Orleans. I'm going in order to learn about human suffering with an insufferable name—leprosy.

Even before leaving New Orleans's airport for Carville, I was able to pick out, from the usual airport crowd, the missionaries waiting for the Carville bus. It was a good opportunity to meet some of my fellow students in the American Leprosy Mission's training course and to shorten the four-hour wait until the bus arrived.

On the darkened bus heading for Carville, I sat with a young doctor who had spent the past two and a half years in Thailand under the auspices of the Southern Baptist Mission. Jack Freedon, originally from Texas, was warm and very open. He and his wife had three children under six years of age and one more on the way. This was their first furlough home since their tour of duty began.

Dr. Freedon talked at length and with great affection about his work in Thailand. He told me that Thai means "free" (similar to Liberia, which means "free country"). He spent his first year in Bangkok and then was sent about eighty miles away to a small hospital, which has three other doctors on staff. Leprosy is integrated into the hospital as one of its departments and there is no stigma because it is treated as it should be, like any other illness.

Dr. Freedon's next-door neighbor in Thailand is a man who has suffered from lepromatous leprosy but is now part of his community again, with a large and happy family and a thriving business in town. This is almost unheard-of in some countries where patients are forced into segregation or go into hiding to avoid it.

Jack told me that his first Sunday at the hospital had been memorable. He had arrived to find the attending physician exhausted from an emergency case. Ching Tong (not his real name), a sixteen-year-old local boy of Chinese ancestry, had been injured in an accident while driving a tractor. Both his lungs had collapsed and he was near death when Jack first saw him. He immediately placed tubes through to each lung and performed a tracheotomy.

He worked frantically for hours to keep Ching Tong alive. During the next few days he stayed with him as much as possible, and a warm relationship developed between them. After the boy recovered, Dr. Freedon asked his parents if Ching Tong could live with him so that he could receive a proper education, which they couldn't afford. It was agreed, and everyone concerned was very happy.

Dr. Freedon spoke also of his role as doctor-missionary and the need for change in the church's approach. He said that he was taught to preach, convert, and heal, and to forge ahead without "listening," but Christ didn't mean for it to be that way at all. He feels a missionary should help but not try to change things.

The hospital is known as Carville, taking its name from the city of its location. It is seventy miles northwest of New Orleans, built into a curve of the Mississippi River. When I first entered its gates, I was surprised to find majestic old structures in an idyllic setting. It was certainly not what I had thought the national leprosarium would look like. Some of the buildings were relics of the site's past as a plantation of the Old South. The hospital building itself was rather unusual. It was designed with corridors hundreds of feet in length, connecting to all the departments, the Protestant and Catholic chapels, and the patients' cottages and dormitories. Flowering trees and shrubs kept these screened corridors cool and fragrant. At all intersections there were racks for bicycles, these being the main form of transportation within the massive structure. Old-fashioned wheelchairs, circa World War One, moved quickly, manipulated by chest-high hand pedals, and they kept pedestrians alert.

The seminar participants were assigned to various smaller buildings on the hospital's perimeter. I was sent to a charming old house, the Bachelor Officer's Quarters, known as the BOQ, where I shared a room with Lavinia Holcomb. Lavinia, a midwestern missionary of the Evangelical Lutheran Church, had been working at Iambi, Tanzania, about two hundred miles south of Kilimanjaro. She had been the only American woman there since 1956. Her hospital, under the direction of a German doctor, had been caring for more than 2500 leprosy patients. I was curious about her life in Africa. Lavinia told me she worked hard.

"I am a nurse twenty-four hours a day, and I am a missionary twenty-four hours a day," she said, almost without emotion. She lived removed from civilization; when her mother died in Minnesota, it had taken her father three days to get word to her by radio. During her mourning period, the tribespeople came by the hundreds every day to sit with her and pat her to show their sympathy. She said the love and comfort they provided was overwhelming.

We attended an introductory briefing given by the training director. He explained that apart from its medical aspects, leprosy is regarded as a social and psychological entity that affects the patient's relationships to family, community, and the health authorities.

"It is a misunderstood disease," he told the gathering, "evoking fear out of all proportion to its contagiousness or severity. It is probably without parallel in the mental and physical distress it causes to its victims and to society at large."

Most of the people attending the seminar had already been involved in leprosy-related work; I was the only lay person in the group. I spoke at length with Dr. Aletta Bell who was working in India. She'd been studying me for a couple of days and finally just came over and asked me if I was a missionary. She said I really stuck out like a sore thumb among the sturdily built ladies in their sleeveless shifts. She was fascinated by the possibility that children of leprosy patients could find homes in receptive societies. She couldn't believe that there were such adoptive parents.

Jewell Olson, a middle-aged registered nurse with many years of experience in the Congo, talked to me about her work at a general hospital that dealt mostly with leprosy patients. American aid was vitally important in the area, particularly foodstuffs. Powdered milk was highly prized, as well as bulgur and corn meal. The hospital staff prescribed the milk for infants suffering from malnutrition, but when the family felt the baby had had enough, the remaining milk was carefully rationed among the other family members.

The lectures were long and intense, as they had to be; there was so much to cover in a very short time. I was certainly impressed with the hospital in its role as a training center and could well understand the need to keep such a facility funded. The dedication and brilliance of the doctors and the devotion of the research people and auxiliary personnel had a profound effect on the American personnel who were going abroad to work and who needed up-to-date information in order to deal with leprosy and its ramifications. In 1973, however, President Ford's administration was pondering the fate of USPHS hospitals throughout the United States, and we could feel the undercurrent of pessimism at Carville about the future.

During a break, an Indian doctor in a sari approached me, inquiring where my mission was. Teasing, I replied, "New York." She smiled and introduced herself as Dr. Arole. As we chatted, she described an encounter with a group of student nurses in the main building; they had waited for her to catch up to them in the hallway so that she could open the doors. They were afraid to touch anything. They also refused to eat in the hospital cafeteria, bringing their own lunch. Until she said this, I hadn't given the idea any thought. However, I noticed we were frequently reminded to wash our hands with the strong brown soap available in the washrooms. I began to feel slightly queasy. But as the day progressed and I learned more about the disease, my discomfort vanished, replaced by compassion for victims of leprosy who are confronted with so much public ignorance.

Another speaker was a Korean doctor who worked in Ethiopia. I introduced myself to Ye Kun Song, who knew Father Lee, and we discussed the adoption of Korean children whose parents were seriously ill. He agreed that when the prognosis for the parents' recovery was poor, adoption was a viable alternative. He felt that although it would be ideal to place such children within their extended family, this was not possible in Korea. The stigma was so pervasive that relatives would not be willing to put their social status in jeopardy by taking such a child into their home. This was exactly what Father Lee had told me.

"Removing the children from their homeland is not a problem in their situation," he said. "When you think about it, all they ever really see of their culture is the sky overhead."

I asked Dr. Song about the possibility of the children contracting leprosy in the future. I had learned there was a three- to five-year incubation period. He said that if the adoptive parents were made fully aware of the child's background, the disease could be treated early and successfully if it should manifest itself. However, since their parents had been on medication prior to their births, he felt it unlikely that any of the children would develop the disease.

One evening, after a discussion of the work of women doctors abroad, I had a long talk with Mrs. Nell Chinchen of Liberia. She told me that out in the bush country where she works, the culture is rather primitive. When a mother dies in childbirth, the baby is considered an "evil spirit" and is taken out into the forest and left to perish. Mrs. Chinchen had been gathering these babies and secretly bringing them into the hospital. Because of their history, they were not likely to be adopted locally, and she asked me about the possibilities of finding homes in the United States for them. She went on to tell me how very beautiful the Liberian babies were. A badly crippled young Brazilian patient, overhearing our conversation, said plaintively, "All healthy creatures are beautiful."

Sitting in a straight, hard chair for long lectures was tough on my back; I spoke to Dr. Paul Brand about my problem. He was an eminent hand surgeon and the head of rehabilitation at Carville. He sent me upstairs to the physical therapists, who would make me a cervical collar to provide temporary help. The therapists both left their office to find what was needed, and I suddenly realized that I wasn't alone in the room. A patient was stretched out on an examining table, strapped to an electronic device. His face, ravaged by Hansen's disease, looked stretched and burned. His fingers were gnarled and his legs had been amputated. I apologized for interrupting his treatment, but he had overheard the conversation about the pain in my back and he very eloquently told me how sorry he was that I was having such bad pain and how much he hoped that I would soon feel better.

During free time one day I walked along the swollen Mississippi with Sister Doctor Marlene, an American black woman who was a medical doctor and a novice in the Catholic church. The water level had risen to seven or eight feet above the hospital grounds. River inspectors rode by every so often in their jeeps, stopping to add sandbags to the levee. We watched them with interest and also enjoyed seeing the foot-long alligators snapping their jaws at bugs along the river's edge.

Marlene's mission work was in Ghana, where she had tried to teach the people about proper nutrition. She told me that getting them to change their traditional patterns was very difficult.

"In Ghana," she said, "the women are the farmers. During the planting season pagan sacrificial rites are performed on animals and small fetishes are carefully fashioned and placed out in the fields. This is done to insure a good harvest."

Marlene saw the opportunity to challenge this tradition by simultaneously planting her own garden without rituals. She borrowed a book about local vegetables and selected some easy-growing varieties. Every eye was on her as she set about her task. She worked under the hot African sun in her flowing white robe, turning the soil, preparing it with fertilizer, and sowing the seeds. After a long day at the hospital, she carried heavy buckets of water uphill from a nearby stream to keep the ground moist. Meanwhile, the pagan rites continued, and the delicately formed fetishes stood silhouetted around the edges of the fields.

A faint green hue began to appear in long rows on the large tracts of farmland, but everyone's attention was on Sister Doctor Marlene's little patch of ground. The days passed, but her seeds did not grow like the others. Not a single green sprout emerged from the carefully-tended earth. She inspected the ground each day with growing disappointment, aware of the green fields around her. "My failure did not surprise anyone," she said, philosophical about the experience, "but it certainly taught me to mind my own business."

One early morning, high winds lashed at the frail building where I slept, waking me before dawn. Lavinia slept right through it. Unable to go back to sleep, I took a towel and headed for the public bathroom down the hall. Two free-standing tubs occupied the center of the room, surrounded by urinals and toilet cubicles. I pulled the drab gray shower curtain full circle and settled into nice hot water, listening to the whirling and whistling sounds of the storm. Soon I heard footsteps approaching and two men's voices. I had mistakenly assumed the bathroom was reserved for women (though the urinals should have made my error clear). I lay quietly in the tub, not daring to make a sound until the men completed their morning toilette and left without discovering my presence. Had anyone suggested, only a few months before, that I would be taking a bath in a public bathroom at a leprosarium, I would have thought that person was out of her mind.

The course included a discussion of the use of drugs in treating leprosy. I learned that the most widely used drug was dapsone, also known as DDS. Inexpensive to produce and usually distributed without charge, the drug prevents contagion after three months. (Newer, more expensive drugs are now available that can produce complete cures in a shorter time.) However, only a small percentage of the estimated fifteen million people who had leprosy were being treated. The stigma is so destructive that they were reluctant to step forward and admit their illness. In many instances, the stigma is actually worse than the disease itself. Leprosy, or Hansen's disease, is caused by bacteria similar to the one that causes tuberculosis. The leprosy bacteria attack the skin and nerves of victims. With early detection and treatment, however, most patients can be cured and therefore avoid deformity.

During a lunch break I sat next to a third-generation missionary doctor, Birch Rambo. He had been working in Zaire at a hospital about seven hundred miles inland; communication was almost impossible in that part of Zaire, because political tension had led the government to forbid using short-wave radios. I was surprised to learn that slavery still existed in Africa. Dr. Rambo found it hard to understand why African Americans embraced the Muslim faith and took on Muslim names, since, he said, it was the Muslims who were the African slave traders.

Every evening the patients, staff, and guests went to church. I alternated between the Catholic and Protestant services, enjoying both of them. At one Catholic mass I heard a sermon given by a priest who was a patient at Carville. He made the sign of the cross with his deformed claw hand and told us he had contracted the disease while working at a colony in Africa. "I thought I was indispensable," he admitted, "but God gave me leprosy to prove that I wasn't."

DEPARTMENT OF HEALTH, EDUCATION, AND WELFARE

PUBLIC HEALTH SERVICE

This certifies that

MRS. BERNICE GOTTLIEB

has satisfactorily completed a training program in

LEPROSY

at ___UNITED STATES PUBLIC HEALTH SERVICE HOSPITAL___
CARVILLE, LOUISIANA

from ___26 April 1973___ to ___2 May 1973___

conducted by

___UNITED STATES PUBLIC HEALTH SERVICE HOSPITAL___

Frank N. Kanatani, R.P.S.,M.P.H.
Chief, Training Branch

John R. Trautman, M.D.
Director

PHS-3344-1 (Rev.4-64)

Bernice's certificate for completing the U.S. Public Health Service's Training Program in Leprosy, April 1973.

After the service some of the women were inspired to talk about how they had found God. They became emotional and tearful as they described the experience. One of them finally gave in to her curiosity and asked what my religion was. When I said I was Jewish, she was surprised that I attended the church services. "Can you actually get a religious experience at a Catholic or Protestant service?" she asked. As the other women moved in closer to listen, I said that I still held fast to my childhood belief that God listened to my prayers no matter where I said them.

Entries from my Carville diary:

April 28

Some of the people who attend the ninety-some seminars given here during the year apparently have many fears to overcome in order to participate. Of course they are mostly inexperienced student nurses who, as part of their training, come to see the facilities of the hospital. Our lecturer explained that he has often had to grasp doorknobs for them as they will not touch anything, nor will they eat or sleep here. One nurse who had to stay overnight came with her own sleeping bag so she wouldn't have to use the linens. This is the kind of ignorance that has to be overcome. Though the mechanics of leprosy transmission is still under study, we learned that this type of contact is quite harmless. In the seventy-five years of existence of this hospital, not one person, doctors or other personnel, has ever contracted the disease. Of course, for the missionaries present, who often work under the worst possible conditions, stories of this type of naive fear bring down the house!

A Brazilian evangelist, Jorge de Macedo, told us during the afternoon about his work in the Amazon jungle. He said that there are half a million people with Hansen's disease on record in Brazil but that he believes the actual figure is closer to a million. As more roads are built through the jungle and as more communication is established, he has found more villages where leprosy is a major health problem. There are thirty leprosaria in Brazil, some with as many as two thousand patients. There is heavy, enforced segregation, which sends many sick people into hiding for fear of separation from their loved ones. Because of this, many who would benefit from early detection and treatment infect household contacts because they are not receiving medication. Jorge is part of a major public education program, one of whose goals is to eradicate the word "leper." His organization is called CERPHA (Commissão Evangélica de Reabilitação de Pacientes de Hanseniase).

Reverend Eugene Evans and his wife Cleo are working in the central highlands of Vietnam, near Pleiku. Individuals with leprosy are totally shunned and isolated in this area. When deformities begin to appear, they are forced to leave their homes and villages. Evans told us about a boy named Krot in a neighboring community. Krot is an orphan and when the villagers discovered that he had leprosy, they decided that the solution was to burn him alive in an ancient ritual. They held a religious ceremony and pre-burial rite during which time poor Krot was forced to drink an intoxicant derived from local plants. They had just started tying him up when a group of missionaries and hospital officials (who had been alerted) came and interrupted the ceremony. He was taken to the hospital and it was discovered that he also had tuberculosis. He is now under treatment for both diseases and will soon be well. But what future can Krot have in such a hostile environment?

The children are not allowed to attend the public schools if their parents have leprosy. The American soldiers stationed outside of Pleiku were saddened to hear this and built them a lovely schoolhouse. After the building was completed, they also built a dispensary for the patients. Reverend Evans cannot praise them enough for the constant help and comfort they have given the patients.

Rats are everywhere. The people sleep on the floor, and because their hands and feet are insensitive to pain, the rats gnaw on them and they cannot protect themselves. A major campaign was launched to bring cats into the village and so far it seems to be working out well.

A nurse, Mildred Ade, who also works in the central highlands of Vietnam, told us about the two Polynesian tribes she ministers to. She said they are quite different from the Vietnamese in general appearance. They are a gentle, caring people, and frequently after bombing raids would go out and gather those babies and children whose parents were dead. They've adopted hundreds of these children into their families and tribes. She told us, "Along with their first Dapsone pill, I give them the Gospel of Jesus Christ."

Mildred was showing us slides of her village and suddenly a slide appeared of a group of smiling young American nurses. Mildred suddenly couldn't speak. When she regained her composure, she explained that she hadn't realized that this slide was among the others. These nurses, she said, all newly arrived from the United States, had been murdered by the Vietcong along with two doctors while Mildred was working in the field. She returned to the hospital to find parts of their mutilated bodies strewn about.

Elizabeth Walton, a registered nurse with white hair and the palest blue eyes, told us she was the entire medical department when she first started her leprosy work in 1950 at Katara, India, a hundred miles west of Nagpur and about five hundred miles from Bombay. She has had a great deal of experience and told us of the importance of watching the patients swallow their pills. Otherwise, they do what is known as "palming." They pretend to swallow but keep the pill in their hand. If they must, they will put the pill on their tongue and keep it there until it is assumed they have swallowed. When they leave the dispensary, they sell the pills. Untouched pills are called "hard-edged" and sell for more money; if they have been in a patient's mouth, they are called "soft-edged." Similarly, Dr. Margaret Brand, an ophthalmologist who worked in India for fifteen years and is now on the Carville staff with her husband Paul, told us how her patients would receive eye drops for a variety of painful problems and save them for their water buffalo.

April 29
Today we heard field reports from most of the countries represented by the missionaries attending the seminar. We spoke about Dapsone and other drugs and of the ideal solution, which is to prevent the disease by correcting the genetic defect that makes the individual susceptible in the first place. Of course, until further experiments are successfully completed with an animal model, this is still a dream. Meanwhile, the armadillo, a funny nine-banded shelled creature about the size of a cat, is the only animal to ever have a case of induced leprosy. The great researcher Dr. Eleanor E. Storrs, in collaboration with Dr. Waldemar Kirscheimer of Carville, accomplished this marvelous breakthrough in 1971.

In the evening a vesper service was held at the side of the lovely lake on the hospital grounds where boats with foot pedals, seeming from another era, moved slow-motion through the water. Father Jerome, the Catholic priest at Carville, drove me down the hill to the services. On the way he asked me if I would like to have him spray me when we got to the lake. I said, "Sure, why not?," really believing he meant holy water. When we got out of the car, he took out a can of 6-12 mosquito repellent.

The service was beautiful and ecumenical. Patients and visitors alike look forward to this annual event. Dr. Paul Brand led the service and he talked about Daniel and the origin of the word "orientation," which means facing the east. The sun was setting toward the end of the service and we left, clapping our hands and singing "Ay-ay-men."

Chapter 5. The Right Parents

After returning home from Carville, I spent most of the rest of 1973 working on the program, now called Outreach. The name had come to me when Westchester County's Department of Social Services first told me they didn't "reach out" to foreign children.

An oversized envelope from Korea arrived and I opened it eagerly. It contained case histories and photographs of the eight children who had been chosen by Father Lee; the documents had been prepared by Social Welfare Society, the same Korean agency that had handled Susannah's overseas paperwork.

I spread the color photographs across the surface of my desk. The healthy, glowing faces in front of me were a contrast to the pictures of orphans I was accustomed to seeing. These children were loved, and they looked it. The youngest, Hee Kyung Cho, still an infant, had a two-year-old sister named Mee Kyung. Hae Suk Chin was not yet two, and her sister Suk was four. Sang Kook Choi, the only boy, was ten, and his sister Hwa Soon was a year younger. Ae Sook

Song, the oldest of the children, was twelve. The last girl, unrelated to her, was eight-year-old Mi Yun Lee. The three pairs of siblings would remain together, of course. I decided to do the same with the unrelated girls. They would be a source of strength to one another that way. Two children would go to each of four families.

I studied the list of interested families that I had compiled, grateful that almost two hundred had come forward. The rumor about the availability of the children, which had spread quickly through the adoption grapevine, had actually started in a rather unlikely manner. A group of would-be adoptive parents with a focus on white infants had invited me to be a guest speaker at one of their functions. Because of the shortage of American babies, they were now looking into various options and wanted information on Korean adoption. Although I was aware of their restrictions, I was so excited about Outreach that I decided to talk about it anyway. I felt there was always a possibility someone in the group would respond.

However, the concept of adopting leprosy patients' children was too far out for this group. They were so shocked by my description of the program that most of the audience walked out before I finished my brief talk. Those remaining expressed their disbelief to me afterwards. But word got out after this rather inauspicious introduction of my program to the public, and other, more sympathetic families besieged me for information.

In my search for parents, I looked for those with the ability to accept a surrogate role. I felt they might have to deal with divided loyalties on the children's part. Not everyone can overcome their possessiveness and adopt a child who has already bonded with living, devoted parents. After all, an important element of Outreach was ongoing communication with the children's biological parents through letters and tapes and the understanding that should the children wish to return to Korea at any time, they would be free to do so, either temporarily or permanently. In addition, it would take a certain maturity to deal with the children's exposure to leprosy. The adoptive parents' understanding was imperative, but they also had to enlist their families' and neighbors' support. And they had to be able to give assurance that the children posed no danger to anyone.

After personal interviews with many parents, I focused on four families who had shown particular sensitivity both to the plight of the biological parents and to leprosy victims in general. Arlene Richards was my first choice for the program. She was thirty-five, single, and had been turned down by other adoption agencies for this reason. I liked her immediately. She was bright, sensitive, and warm. She held a well-paid position in the Department of Health, Education and Welfare and had her own very comfortable home in D.C. She had recently adopted a two-year-old girl from Vietnam, and I believed she would make a superb parent for Suk and Hae Suk. Their mother had suffered from chronic depression since having a leg amputated and had attempted suicide several times. Their father, who had taken over their care, was going blind. When I read their medical history, I was reminded of the first time I had seen leprosy patients at Carville. I hadn't really known what to expect. Surprisingly, many of those with severe cases looked only as if they had chronic skin rashes. Some, who had not been diagnosed or treated early, had developed deformities because of nerve damage that especially affected their limbs. But absolutely no one looked as horribly damaged as Hollywood movies such as "Papillon" or "Ben Hur" had led us to believe.

The Korean government had strict rules for citizens of other countries who wished to adopt their children. Single parents were generally disallowed, as were families with five or more children. There was also an age limit of fifty for adoptive parents. However, I had been informed that all of these restrictions could be waived in special cases. I felt our program qualified for such waivers and kept this in mind when selecting the next family. Peter and Betty Edwards were English-born and just past fifty when they applied. They had two grown biological children and had previously adopted three Korean orphans. Peter was an automobile salesman, and Betty, a tall freckled redhead, was a part-time clerk at Macy's department store. They were unusual, special people, and I was very pleased to work with them. After reviewing the remaining case histories, we agreed that the two unrelated girls were perfect for their family.

Through this family I met another interested couple, John and Fran Daley. They had five biological children, ranging in age from three to twelve, and they wished to adopt two more. This would be the third family requiring special waivers; I hoped that my expectations of gaining such permission were realistic. The Daleys seemed an ideal couple, however, and I felt that Sang Kook and Hwa Soon would find an excellent home with them. John was a systems analyst for an aerospace company, and he and Fran were active in the Catholic encounter movement. This would surely please Father Lee. The first two families, Arlene Richards and the Edwardses, were Protestant, but each was willing to further the children's Catholic education. Arlene, in fact, offered to convert if it was critical. Father Lee was happy that she had offered, but he didn't ask her to do so.

Like the Daleys, the last couple, Louis and Janet Martino, were Catholic; they were also the youngest of the families. Louis was a New York City police officer, and he and Janet had two biological children. Of course, the final decision on acceptance would have to come from a licensed adoption agency who would perform a home study for all the prospective parents.

I did not consider more than these eight children initially. If the general legislation had been passed, it would have allowed unlimited numbers of healthy children of people with leprosy into the country.

But for now, my focus, and that of Father Lee, remained only on this small group.

In February 1974 I started planning my trip to Korea for the following month. Fred agreed to join me, which gave me a great sense of security. I felt it was essential for us to meet the Korean parents in order to be certain they understood the ramifications of giving their children in adoption.

It was almost two years since I had first met Father Lee. My family was changing and growing. My father had agreed to come live with us now that he was getting older. Susannah had had her seventh birthday, Richard was thirteen, and Peter had already finished his first semester of college. I was fortunate to have been able to do my volunteer work at home and spend so much quality time with them. But they took my presence for granted, as kids are apt to do. When I told them about my forthcoming trip to Korea, Richard said, "The more you do for other children, the less you do for us."

Ordinarily I would have challenged him on a remark like that. But I had a funny feeling this time that Richard could be right. There was a foreboding in place of my usual enthusiasm and confidence.

TAISSA had officially agreed to be the cooperating child placement agency for Outreach. I asked their executive director, William H. Taylor (known as Mac), if I could possibly be an "escort." This meant that in return for a paid ticket, I would escort a group of orphans from Korea to the United States. Mac agreed, as they were always looking for volunteers for this service. There were five children ready to emigrate, requiring two escorts, so Fred's ticket would also be paid. Since we were supporting Outreach financially at the time, this was welcome news. Mac asked that we stop in Hawaii on the way to Korea. Their fund-raising division, WAIF (World Adoption International Foundation), would be interested in what I was planning to do, he thought, and the Hawaiian section of this group was an active one.

When she heard about the Outreach program, Margie asked if she could cover the story of our visit to Korea for NBC. I agreed, as I felt it would help create public support for the children of St. Lazarus and would also bring the plight of thousands of such children to national attention.

Chapter 6. St. Lazarus Village: March 1974

On the way to Korea:

Everyone who visits Molokai must experience the excitement that we felt. The small propeller plane noisily approached the island, which lies between Oahu and Maui. Kalaupapa, the leprosy settlement, is a narrow strip of land at sea level on the north central edge of Molokai. It is where Father Damien, the Catholic priest, did his remarkable work more than one hundred years ago.

We landed on a small airstrip, met by warm breezes smelling of sweet Hawaiian flowers. Pete and Richard, the island's tour guides and residents of Kalaupapa, greeted us with leis, the traditional Hawaiian welcome. Pete was living out his days at this settlement, having been on the island for most of his life. Richard was sent here in his junior year of college and had never gone home again. Pete's damaged hands, with stubs for fingers, handled the wheel of his jeep very well as we rode, the fringed canvas roof protecting us from the scorching sun.

Although the Kalaupapa community had its comforts, such as a small hospital and a PX, a strong feeling of change emanated from the massive bulldozers and survey equipment that the government had brought in. The settlement was being phased out and would eventually become a state park.

The patients lived in small cottages, built in neat rows, and there was little visual evidence that this settlement differed dramatically from other middle-class Hawaiian communities. A huge cross, which can be seen for miles, dominated a mountain looking out to sea. From the plateau, we drank in scenes of indescribable beauty. Far below, we saw a pond that looked like pea soup. Richard said that legend held the pond to be bottomless. Mysterious disappearances of a number of island people over the years were attributed to the evil spirits lurking within it.

Richard was a bitter man. He told us why the dogs on the island were known as "island babies"; it was because the government did not allow new generations to be born in Kalaupapa. He said that recently a woman was sent to the mainland hospital to deliver her baby. When her husband telephoned the hospital, he was told that no such person was registered. Worst of all, she could not return to Kalaupapa with her baby. She had to decide whether to remain on the mainland with her child or leave the baby behind and rejoin her husband. "Her decision was to return to Kalaupapa, with empty arms and an emptier heart," he said.

We saw one of the churches built by Father Damien, with its small graveyard. Damien's actual remains had been removed to his birthplace in Belgium, Pete told us. "They take everything from us," he lamented, "even Damien's coffin."

Father Damien's memorial, surrounded by a handsomely turned wrought iron fence, has a large iron cross covered with fresh flower leis. I was moved to tears at the sight of his name on the cross and bent down to pick up a stone as a remembrance of the moment. Pete watched me and understood. "Just a minute," he said. "I'll get you a much better one." He climbed over the fence and from the gravesite itself picked up a small, round black marble stone. I put both stones into my travel bag.

Father Damien's grave at Kalaupapa.

From Molokai, the journey continued to Japan and then on to South Korea. Fred and I were met at Kimpo Airport by Father Lee, who drove us directly to St. Lazarus Village in his red Volkswagen. Suwon, where St. Lazarus is located, is in Anyang Province, about fifteen or twenty miles south of Seoul. We drove along a modern highway, which had not been in existence during my trip six years earlier when I had found Susannah. Tall masonry walls on either side hid some of the less attractive sights along the way. Every now and then wide expanses of frozen farmland were visible behind the wall, stretching as far as we could see. It was bitter cold for March, with temperatures well below freezing, accompanied by a pervasive dampness.

Along the sidewalks beside the highway, women wearing traditional hanboks carried babies and young children on their backs. Children too carried younger siblings the same way. Many bicycles were piled five or six feet high with merchandise destined for sale along the highways and in village marketplaces. Often a man pulled the bicycle or rode it, while a woman pushed from behind. There were also oxen pulling wagons, some loaded with children and some with vegetables or other farm products on their way to market.

The entrance to St. Lazarus Village faced the highway. Emblazoned on either side of its imposing masonry walls were the words "The Seeds of Our Love Will Grow." The winding dirt road, partially paved, forked after fifty yards or so, and we took the right turn, leading to the whitewashed buildings of Father Lee's quarters. Beyond, the road continued to the various service structures and patient dormitories. The left fork, rocky and harder to traverse, led to jerry-built shacks of wood and masonry block; these were chicken and hog houses and a general store, all owned by the self-supporting village residents. The otherwise barren landscape was speckled with brown ceramic kimchee pots (kimchee being the spicy cabbage staple of the Korean diet).

Inside the village, to the left, in the "self-supporting" section, people had been given parcels of land to build their houses. These were not positive cases, but "burned out" ones who eked out a living by farming and raising chickens and hogs; they led a substandard existence similar to that in many ordinary poor villages in the area. Their water supply was a pump, and the water was polluted. Merchants occasionally came into the village with carts and bicycles to sell wares.

An outside vendor's cart arriving at St. Lazarus Village.

A typical house in the self-supporting section consisted of one or two rooms, sparsely furnished. The sleeping mats and quilts were kept behind a curtained area of the room, and the cold winters were tolerable because of the floor, which had clay pipes underneath. These pipes were directly connected to the stove in the kitchen, and when something was cooking, the heat went through the pipes, heating the floor where the residents both sit and sleep. The only decoration in some of these homes was a religious picture.

Certain areas of the village were off-limits to patients and other villagers. Except for one of the nuns who lived there and the two young women, Raiko Kabusaki and Young-ok, who worked for Father Lee, no resident of St. Lazarus was allowed into his quarters, which consisted of a bedroom, bathroom, kitchen, and living/dining room. His office was off to one side, but much of his work was done in the living room where there was both a fireplace and a charcoal stove. On one wall of his office was a padlocked glass box. He was a charismatic speaker, and in many countries, women took off their wedding rings and diamonds and handed them to him because they were eager to do something to help his cause; the padlocked box was full of pieces of jewelry. His national awards and medals decorated the walls, and pictures of him with important Korean dignitaries were everywhere.

When we arrived, we relaxed in the priest's study and talked about our Hawaiian experience. I asked Father Lee whether he had ever been to Molokai. He said he had gone some years before and was planning another trip. "You see, we are building a church here at St. Lazarus," he said, "replacing the small chapel we are presently using." He pointed out an artist's rendering of the new church building. "For sentimental reasons," he continued, "I wish to return to Molokai so that I can take a stone from Father Damien's grave and cement it near the cornerstone of the new church, which is being dedicated to him. "

Fred and I exchanged glances, and I dug into the recesses of my travel bag. After some groping, I found the black marble stone that Pete had given me in Kalaupapa. Placing it in my outstretched palm, I gave it to Father Lee, explaining how I had come by it. He was astonished, staring at the stone as if it had appeared through some sort of miracle. Then he began to laugh heartily and we joined in.

"Providence has brought us together, Bernice," he said, "and I truly thank God for it!"

We accepted Father Lee's invitation to spend the night at St. Lazarus, sleeping on a concrete floor in a basement room in the nuns' dormitory. The floor mats were surprisingly comfortable with their crisp linens and goose down quilts, but the room itself had no heat and it was freezing. The small sink in one corner of the room offered only cold water. I was too cold to remove my clothes. Instead, as my stoic husband undressed, I put his clothes on over my own. We both slept well, however, anticipating our first meeting with the children in the morning.

Sounds from the kitchen woke us before dawn. Upstairs we were greeted by two nuns and also by Raiko and Young-ok. Raiko, who was Japanese, was fluent in English. When she saw us, she flew into the kitchen, emerging in a few minutes with a tray of hamburgers covered with a mountain of fried onions. "I have made you an American breakfast," she said proudly, as all the faces in the room broke into pleased grins. We forced the hamburgers down, regretfully forgoing the Korean repast that was artfully laid out.

I got to know Raiko quite well. She had heard Father Lee speak in Japan and was so interested and impressed that she determined to devote herself to helping people with leprosy. She came to Korea to work for Father Lee when she was in her early twenties. Because she was a linguist, speaking several languages fluently, he made her his assistant with a desk in his office. When I met her seven years later, she was close to thirty. She had labored long and hard for Father Lee at St. Lazarus for only a small stipend. She stayed at the village most of the time, helping the patients when she could and helping Father Lee all the time. When she started working for him, there were no nuns at St. Lazarus, which meant that she took on many responsibilities. She dressed the patients' wounds and catered to Father Lee in every possible way, entertaining his guests, carrying out the administrative duties when he was away, and generally devoting herself completely to her work. She played the guitar and sang songs from all over the world in a charming voice with a great deal of expression. She cared little about her appearance, but in her plainness there was great beauty.

Dr. Lee, a young Korean, started coming to the village once a month with a mobile unit and other volunteer doctors and dentists. He often saw Raiko there and began to admire her dedication. In 1974, while Fred and I were in Korea, he asked her out to dinner. She didn't know what to wear, so we rummaged through the clothes I had brought. She was tiny, but we pinned up a skirt to fit her, and I gave her a pretty sweater. Then I helped her fix her hair. She came back glowing.

Raiko kept in touch with me as their romance grew. Dr. Lee told her he had met so many selfish women who just cared about themselves and how they looked and who only wanted to marry wealth; he had never met anyone like her. Father Lee was very upset and tried to discourage the relationship, but they were in love and decided to get married. This was not as easy as it sounds, because the Koreans and the Japanese don't get along well together; the Japanese occupation of Korea from 1910 to 1945 left a lot of bitter feelings on both sides. So both Dr. Lee's family and Raiko's father in Tokyo (her mother had died), as well as Father Lee, were against the marriage. But their love for each other won out and they were married in the cathedral of Seoul. Father Lee refused to attend the wedding. He was very unhappy to lose her; I think he secretly loved her. Raiko sent me a photo taken on her wedding day; she looked more beautiful than I had ever imagined. Her beauty was there all the time, waiting to be brought out by this wonderful story of love. They now have a son and live somewhere in Korea.

That first morning, I kept thinking how good it was to be back in Korea. I looked around me with affection at the faces of Father Lee, the two shy nuns, and Raiko and Young-ok. The black potbellied stove that burned charcoal briquettes took away our chill during breakfast. Afterwards, we bundled into our down jackets and accompanied Father Lee to the chapel. The church bells were ringing; it was time for six o'clock mass.

The elderly blind bell ringer, bent and disfigured, was standing in the open bell tower, pulling on the long rope. The melancholy tones echoed throughout the valley. The tall, delicate structure afforded him little protection from the wind, but his task occupied him and

Raiko and Dr. Jong Wook Lee, December 1976.

he seemed oblivious. We entered the chapel through the back door and were shown to small chairs in an alcove, next to where the nuns were seated. Except for the sparsely furnished altar, the chapel was bare, almost pristine. The congregation started arriving, walking in their stocking feet on the wide-planked wooden floor, their shoes neatly stacked on wooden shelves at the chapel's entrance.

The women were on one side of the room, their heads covered with white lace handkerchiefs, the men on the other, heads bowed low. Some brought cushions, others knelt directly on the bare floor. From where we sat, we could see that most of the people were bandaged and hobbled in on crutches. When a man got up to light a candle, I approached Father Lee, asking if I could do the same. It was the ninth anniversary of my mother's death, I told him. I explained that had I been home, I would have lit a candle the evening before, which would burn until sunset the following day. Father Lee listened, then thoughtfully performed an anniversary mass in her memory, the patients chanting and singing the prayers for Mother.

Village residents in the chapel.

Suk and Hae Suk were the only children in the chapel. I recognized them from their photographs and was thrilled to see them in person. They sat huddled near the unlit charcoal stove and I had to control the urge to cross the room and embrace them. When the service was over, it was they who ran to me, chattering away in Korean.

Outside, in the snow, little Hee Kyung and Mee Kyung were waiting for us with their parents, Mr. and Mrs. Cho. The younger child was tied to their mother's back, her sister clinging shyly to their father's leg. The young parents were very handsome, but as they drew closer, I was struck by the pain in their faces. After all, I would be taking their children away. Before meeting them, I had intellectualized this whole experience and the fantasy of rescue, unable truly to comprehend the extent of their sacrifice. Now the pain became clearer.

We walked together along the hillside, as snow came down heavily and clung to our faces and clothes. Suk and Hae Suk walked near us, stopping to make snowballs. Curious villagers watched from their windows, their curtains held aside. The mountains, barely visible in the snow fog, were steep and barren. Land cultivation had to be done with bench terracing, creating plateaus on which rice and vegetables could be grown. Except for the disabled and positive patients who were under Father Lee's care, most of the nearly four hundred inhabitants had to struggle for subsistence. The previous year had been disastrous. They had lost more than sixty thousand chickens to a poultry disease, leaving many residents without a source of income.

We stopped in front of the building that housed the disabled patients. Mr. Cho invited us inside. His wife, still carrying Hee Kyung on her back, parted the curtains of the closet at one end of the room, removing several floor cushions. All their possessions were contained in that tiny space. The room was small, and they shared a communal kitchen with two other families, including Suk and Hae Suk's parents. A colorful print of the infant Jesus hung crookedly on one wall, a strip of Easter palm tucked behind it. There was no furniture in the room. Mr. Cho's elderly mother, her hanbok covered by a floor-length apron, was grinding red peppers with mortar and pestle.

When they learned of our arrival, Mr. and Mrs. Chin, Suk and Hae Suk's parents, appeared. Mr. Chin was a sensitive and articulate man, his wife withdrawn. Once beautiful, her face was now distorted on one side and she walked with a pronounced limp. I noticed how protective Mr. Chin was of five-year-old Suk, who was using a sharp knife to peel some fruit. Neither he nor his wife were able to manipulate such tools any longer and had taught their small daughters these tasks. But Mr. Chin, nearly blind, leaned closely over his child until the knife was safely put away.

The other families of the adoptive children lived in the self-supporting section of the village. It was expected that we introduce ourselves to the village leader, Chu Song Kwon, before meeting them, so Fred and I walked down the winding road to the south end of the village with Father Lee. On the way he explained that most of the inhabitants were farmers by trade. The pig and chicken farmers, as well as those who grew the rice and vegetables, sold their produce in the city marketplace. This was done by those who had no outward signs of disease.

Father Lee showed us the kitchen where pig food was prepared, the odor so gross we couldn't linger. We passed a medical dispensary that looked in need of paint and repair. It was a long, narrow building with several examination rooms. The patients were queued up at one end where the clinic and pharmacy were located, awaiting the monthly visit of a mobile unit from the Catholic medical center. While his mother watched anxiously, a screaming baby boy, his leg scalded by water from a rice pot, was having the wound dressed by a patient who had learned to take the doctor's place in an emergency.

Villagers waiting at the clinic to see the doctor
during his monthly mobile visit.

Inside the clinic, where a child is being treated for burns from a rice pot.

We walked into the general store where milk, herbs, and canned goods were sold. There were very few items on the shelves, however. The shopkeepers and their son viewed us suspiciously, turning their backs when I used my camera to photograph the store. Father Lee explained that they were planning to leave the village and did not want to be recognized on the outside. A pot and pan vendor, his wares piled high on a three-wheeled bicycle, was trying to make a sale near the water pump where some women had gathered.

Chu Song Kwon was a lean man with a soft voice and delicate features. He invited us into a small meeting room and thoughtfully placed our chairs near the charcoal burner. Several men, who had been in animated conversation when we entered, became silent and rose to greet us. We spent quite a while in the room, but social custom dictated that nothing of substance would be discussed at this first meeting.

After the first night at St. Lazarus, Fred and I stayed at the Ambassador Hotel in Seoul. Margie had arranged for a Korean NBC crew to film our visit to St. Lazarus. But when the crew received the assignment, at first they refused to accept it; they were terrified to enter the village. In Seoul, Fred invited the crew to lunch at the hotel and, after several hours of discussion, convinced them that they would not be in danger.

Once they were persuaded, the NBC crew filmed quite a lot. They took footage of the village and its surrounding landscape, the chapel, and the bell tower with the patient ringing the bell for mass; patients going to church and participating in the service; the chicken house, the hogs and cows, the store and its owners, men working in the fields; the dining room, kitchen, and dispensary; the school and children in classrooms and playground; one of our meetings with Father Lee, Chu Song Kwon, and other village leaders; and some of the children to be adopted and their parents.

NBC planned to air this news clip on April 12, 1974, during its evening news program anchored by John Chancellor. This went ahead as scheduled, even though *The New York Times* scooped NBC by running the Outreach story on their front page on the morning of that same day. Both the television story and the newspaper article generated a great deal of response, most of it very positive.

One day near the end of our visit, we went to the Ministry of Health and Social Affairs, which was in the Unified Government building, part of the government complex of modern office buildings in downtown Seoul. Accompanied by Dr. Shi Ryong Choi, Director of the Chronic Disease Laboratory at Catholic Medical Center, Father Lee, Fred, and I entered the revolving doors of the building to find ourselves surrounded by alert security police with drawn guns. In order to go upstairs for our meeting with Dr. Yu Un Seong, Director of the Bureau of Public Health, we had to obtain written passes at various stations within the lobby.

We first paid a courtesy call on the Minister of Health, a distinguished, formally attired gentleman, and then headed for the Public Health office. Three men, all junior health officials, were waiting and showed us into the meeting room. Dr. Seong, a bespectacled, scholarly-looking man, soon entered and we were introduced. None of the officials spoke English and for the first half hour Father Lee did not translate. I knew he was explaining the purpose of our visit, which was to obtain the release of the children for emigration and the necessary permission to waive the restrictions for qualifying adoptive parents.

At one point the conversation came to a halt and Father Lee asked me a number of questions on behalf of Dr. Seong. It seemed the government had a concern about the adoption of these children that I couldn't have anticipated. They were worried about the publicity this program would receive in the international press.

"South Korea is no longer on its knees," Dr. Seong said. "Tourism and industry are flourishing and the government does not want adverse publicity to hurt our economy. We especially do not wish to be associated with a major leprosy problem," he stressed. "We do have some eighty-seven leprosy colonies here in South Korea, but they are not overcrowded. In fact, there are fewer than eighty thousand inhabitants living in them, and the children's population is fairly limited." He showed me a list of the estimated numbers of healthy children under fourteen years of age living in the colonies and in contrast noted that Brazil had something like half a million people with leprosy.

Dr. Choi, the medical supervisor of the patients and their children at St. Lazarus, explained to Dr. Seong that he had meticulously examined each of the eight children and found them free of disease and generally healthy. He also said that the children's parents had all been under treatment before their birth, making them noncontagious to their offspring. Again, a long period of discussion ensued, sans translation. I looked around the room. The men's expressions were all rather grim. The conversation didn't seem to be going all that well.

Then Dr. Seong and the other three men excused themselves and left the narrow meeting room. Father Lee said nothing to us and just stared down at the floor. I leaned over to him and in a whisper asked how he thought the meeting was going. He said he still felt some uncertainty because one of the men had brought up the possibility that our program could be fodder for North Korean propaganda. The North Koreans were already highly critical of South Korean adoption policies.

When they returned, we sat forward in our seats. Father Lee spoke with the group at length, then everyone but he and Dr. Choi inexplicably burst out laughing. "Well," he said, with a sigh of relief, "I am happy to tell you that after consulting with the Minister of Health, Dr. Seong has granted our request and has also received permission to waive all restrictions that apply to regular adoption."

I was thrilled to hear it and went over to Dr. Seong to thank him. He and his associates were still laughing as we said goodbye.

We could hear them as we walked to the elevator. "What's going on?" I asked Father Lee, as soon as we were out of earshot. "Why in heaven's name are they laughing like that?"

"They are laughing because one of the men said that as far as they are concerned, we can take all of the mikama to America," Father Lee said, raising his eyebrows at us. "All six and one-half thousand of them!"

That night at St. Lazarus, I saw that Father Lee's left hand was wrapped in a thick bandage. I asked him what was wrong, and he told me that he had caught his hand in the revolving door as we entered the Ministry of Health earlier that day; his hand was broken. I couldn't believe that he had sat through the whole day of meetings, translating for us and worrying that the officials would not grant our requests. What amazing strength and resolve he had!

A meeting with the parents and other members of the St. Lazarus community was to be held that evening in the school. The two-room school building at St. Lazarus had been provided by the provincial government to avoid confrontation with those attending the public schools. The lessons at the school included the information that not every child grew up to become a deformed adult with stumps for fingers, a misshapen face, or discolored skin. Some of the older children, especially those with more than average ability, found the education inadequate and secretly attended outside schools. This was accomplished through the help of sympathetic educators, some of whom accepted gifts. But the children had to keep their identities carefully hidden, using false addresses and never inviting any school friends home. They were aware of the fear and prejudice of those on the outside who spat on them, calling them mikama or mundungi. They had heard about the riots in another province when an attempt was made to integrate a school; several people, including children, were reportedly murdered during that incident.

Father Lee with the Chin children.

Some of the children at St. Lazarus Village.

The weather worsened toward evening, the temperature dropping rapidly. It was difficult to walk up the hill to the school, the wind pushing us backwards with each step. When we arrived, chilled to the bone, a large group of people was already waiting, a fire blazing in the stove. Father Lee went into the smaller of the two rooms and emerged with the four children we had been waiting to meet. Hwa Soon and Sang Kook Choi bowed low when we were introduced, as did Ae Sook Song and Mi Yun Lee. All four were splendid, healthy-looking youngsters. Although this was our first meeting, I knew them well from their photographs and histories. The oldest child, Ae Sook, was almost thirteen; she was very shy, keeping her eyes lowered when we spoke. Mi Yun was a cheerful, outgoing nine-year-old who showed how pleased she was to meet us. The Choi children, Hwa Soon, age ten, and Sang Kook, age eleven (the only boy in the group), were notably good-looking and self-assured.

At Father Lee's suggestion, the children left the schoolhouse before the meeting started. We were then introduced to everyone in the room. The parents, many of whom looked older than their years, showed varying signs of leprosy—some perfectly normal-looking, others with claw hands, amputations, and bone absorption of fingers or nose.

A hush came over the gathering as Father Lee got up to speak. Raiko sat between Fred and me in order to translate. "You have asked that I find families in America who will take your children," he said. "Through the grace of God I have met the person who will make this dream possible. However, you must recognize that when you send your children away for adoption, they will belong to the other family. The smaller children may entirely forget their loved ones and even the language we speak here."

He stopped, anticipating questions, but when only silence greeted him, he continued. "You will have to accept that the future, regarding their education, career, and where they will live, whether in the United States or Korea, shall all be a matter of their own choosing and will be out of your hands."

When he had finished speaking, Father Lee asked that I say a few words. I spoke about each of the prospective adoptive families, and how they had willingly agreed to write the parents in Korea, establishing relationships between the two families. "It will be a sharing of love between you," I promised them. "The children must always remember that you are their birth parents and that Korea is their homeland."

They asked about American customs and the communities where their children would live. They asked about the schools and if their children would have to face fear and prejudice in America. They wanted to know if the American families were very rich. Mr. Kwon, the village leader, had been listening to the many questions about the social status of the American families and took issue with the parents on this subject. Facing the group, he pointedly remarked, "We should not concern ourselves with whether the children go to wealthy homes. Our only concern should be that they love our children." This reminded me of something Father Lee had told me; there were several patients at St. Lazarus who had wealthy relatives, but these family members had refused to take the patients' children into their homes or to provide a good education for them.

My thoughts were interrupted by Mr. Cho, Mee Kyung and Hee Kyung's father, who was addressing me. "I am not asking that you promise me anything, Mrs. Gottlieb," he said, "but just give me the hope that when my daughters grow up, if they want to come home, they can." I told him that children do not really belong to anyone and, once grown, are free agents. Mr. Kwon then stood up and summarized the feelings of the parents with the following statement: "We trust Father Lee, we trust Mr. and Mrs. Gottlieb, and we trust the United States of America. Therefore, we will permit our children to leave Korea."

"We are only human," Fred said. "There may be problems and setbacks that we will have to face, but my wife and I give you our word that we will do everything we can to help your children."

The parents' questions about their children's future lives so far away were a heart-rending mix of concerns any parent would express and worries specific to these stigmatized and isolated families. The evening before our departure, Ae Sook's mother took me aside with Raiko in hand to translate.

"I have only one concern about my child," she said. "Ae Sook is almost thirteen years old now and is already a woman. Every month when she is bleeding, I give her soft white rags which I have stitched into pads for her to wear. Afterwards I wash the pads carefully and hang them in the sun to dry. Will her adoptive mother do this for her?"

On almost our last day in Korea, a gathering was arranged for people who helped St. Lazarus by making financial donations in accordance with Korean traditions of charitable giving. These "helpers" came from all walks of life. Father Lee's eloquence and charisma brought them to St. Lazarus once a month for a meeting. When they were seated, Father Lee made a very moving speech about our work with Outreach.

Several hundred thousands of people have visited Korea every year...And thousands of unfortunate children have been adopted to America and European countries from Korea....But among those visiting people, how many people came for helping the children of leprosy patients, and how many of them have been adopted to abroad? Formally none, as long as I remember....

How are leprosy patients' children situated in the society of Korea? They are treated just as not to be existing....Leprosy patients' children are not diseased. And many of their parents have been recovered. In spite of it, they are not accepted into ordinary schools in the town, and the fact that they are the patients' children emerges as a problem in every aspect of their life: marriage, getting jobs and so on, and it stands as a bigger and bigger problem in their way.

...Mrs. Gottlieb, you have been making efforts for them so actively with much concern since the time we got acquainted two years ago....

As you also know, we have some different points. You are an American, and I am a Korean. You are a Judaist, and I am a Catholic. But we have the same philosophy as far as things concern unfortunate people and unfortunate children.

When I think of everything after our first encounter, I cannot but regard it as Our Lord's Providence. This program needs much more of our efforts for the materialization. The seeds, however, have been sown. When we give the water of efforts and cooperation, God will bring these up and make them bear fruits. The realization of our program will not only give happiness to the children and their parents but will also give a good chance of having stimulation and education to the much prejudiced society.

We might have difficult and unexpected obstacles in our way. But let us proceed quietly with a firm determination so that we can give joy to as many children as possible. Your visit, Mr. and Mrs. Gottlieb, it is the first beautiful news of the spring of this year....And we give you many thanks that you have visited this faraway country and we welcome you from the bottom of our heart.

Sooner or later, the seeds of our love will grow.

From left: Father Lee (his broken hand in his pocket), Bernice, Raiko Kabusaki, two Carmelite nuns, a member of the St. Lazarus helpers, Young-ok, and Fred at St. Lazarus Village, March 1974.

I was both honored and touched when I was given a Korean name, Go Soong Ae; I can still picture Martha Yoon, the Chins, and the Chos sitting in the kitchen choosing it. My own name, Bernice, means "victory," and Gottlieb is really two German words that mean "God" and "love." Translated, Go Soong Ae means something close to "Love Conquers All," which seemed a perfect complement to my American name and which also reflected the guiding principle of St. Lazarus Village.

On our way home from Korea, we escorted the five children being adopted by American families through TAISSA. We dropped two off in California, two in Chicago, and one in New York. It was an incredibly emotional experience to share in the happiness and excitement of the waiting adoptive parents. I couldn't wait to have this experience with the children from St. Lazarus.

Chapter 7. A Difficult Search

When we returned from Korea in March 1974, everything seemed to be in place. Four adoptive families were eager to welcome the children; eight children and their parents in Korea were ready for this momentous change in their lives; and their arrival was tentatively scheduled for the following September, only six months away. But some internal difficulties had arisen at TAISSA, the adoption agency that had agreed to handle our adoptions, and they were stalled over the question of working with Outreach.

At the same time, Dr. Bruce Grynbaum, the same doctor who alerted me to the leprosy course given at Carville which he found in a medical journal, introduced me to the head of the Rusk Institute at NYU Medical Center. Grynbaum, a brilliant physician, had worked closely for many years at the Institute with Howard Rusk, the founder, and Dr. Rusk was pleased to meet me and to hear of my plans. Rusk was also chairman emeritus of the American-Korean Foundation and I was thrilled that he arranged for a grant from AKF to support my work.

Dr. Howard Rusk, founder of the Rusk Institute at New York University
Medical Center, chairman emeritus of the American-Korean Foundation,
and the "father" of rehabilitation medicine.

Recognized globally as the father of rehabilitation medicine, Rusk had been inspired by the wounded soldiers he encountered during World War II and had worked out a program of retraining, reconditioning, and psychological readjustment that helped prepare them to return to useful life once again. His dedication to the idea of rehabilitation after injury or illness continued for the rest of his life. I was happy to learn that Hansen's disease also happened to be one of his many medical interests. I admired Dr. Rusk greatly and was touched and flattered when he wrote to me in May 1974, "...I know great good is going to come from your wonderfully conceived program all over the world. Many people will stand to bless you."

Mac Taylor was my contact at TAISSA; now that the American-Korean Foundation was behind me, I thought Mac's nose was a bit out of joint, because he felt he would not have as much input in my plans for the program. We ended up parting ways when TAISSA's board decided that Outreach was too controversial for them. (However, their name was already on record as our cooperating agency, and this later caused me great aggravation and infuriated the powers that be in Washington.) Ironically, much later (in August 1974), Mac Taylor received a letter from Dr. Soo Duk Lim of the Sloan-Kettering Institute for Cancer Research in New York; in it, the doctor apologized for his delayed reply and went on to express complete support for Outreach's plans. He concluded by saying, "The Outreach Program is a unique and ambitious educational project in this field. Subsequently, your assistance in developing this program, to rid the world of this stigma, will be a great contribution to society."

TAISSA's backing out at this stage of the process meant I had to undertake a frantic search for another agency. Arlene Richards had been working with Peirce-Warwick in Washington, D.C., and I made an appointment to meet with their director, Charles Olds. We had a number of meetings, but although he wanted very much to proceed, he ran into opposition from a pediatrician who sat on his board. This doctor was not comfortable with the idea that the children had been exposed to leprosy. After much discussion, Peirce-Warwick declined.

I ran into the same problem with several other agencies, as I traveled across the country searching for one with the courage to help make my program happen. Without a licensed agency, we could not proceed, and the children's expected arrival in September had to be postponed, which made us all very unhappy. At an adoption conference in September at Marylhurst College in Oregon, I met Jack Adams, the director of the Holt Agency in Eugene, and he suggested I drive to Eugene and speak with his associate David Kim and other members of the staff about my plans. Holt was one of the largest international adoption agencies in the country, and I felt hopeful that the children's background would not scare them off.

I drove to Eugene with one of Holt's social workers who had been at the conference. Eleanor Rivers had worked for a while for Holt's operation in Vietnam. She was single, and she told me she had left Vietnam because of a tense situation that developed when she wanted to adopt an orphan she had become attached to. Her supervisor had the child placed with someone else because she didn't approve of any agency personnel, especially those who were unmarried, getting involved with the children they were serving. Although Eleanor expressed bitterness, she remained devoted to the agency—a warm and vital woman.

Eleanor's home was being painted and she was temporarily living at the home of friends in town. They were traveling, and Eleanor invited me to stay with her at their lavishly furnished home. She insisted I use the master bedroom, and I went to drop my bags there before joining her in the kitchen for a snack. The bed looked so inviting. Then, on the bureau, I saw a large, framed photograph of an SS officer, his uniform complete with swastika armband.

"Who owns this house?" I asked Eleanor uncomfortably.

"A lovely German couple. They are good friends of mine."

"Is that your friend's photograph on the bureau?" I asked, goose bumps rising on my arms.

"Look, Bernice," she said defensively. "That was a long time ago. Kurt was never a Nazi, I'm sure of that. He had no choice but to join up like so many others. Take my word for it, they are wonderful people." She smiled.

We said good night, but I had no intention of sleeping in that bed. I took a blanket from the linen closet and slept fitfully on the couch in the living room, without undressing. I felt even the lampshades in that house looked suspicious.

The following morning's meeting was a disaster. First of all, they wanted to see me at 5:00 a.m. Then, when I arrived promptly at 5:00, no one was there and I waited until 6:30 for members of the Holt team to arrive. Finally, it turned out that the Holt agency would not work with a non-Christian; also, Jack Theis, their director in Korea, had reservations about the program. Why hadn't they told me this before I made the trip? I would have to continue my search.

After this disastrous meeting with the Holt agency, Clayton Hagen, one of the best spokespersons for transracial adoption in the United States, tried to lend a hand by recommending Outreach to Children's Home Society of Minnesota (his home state). I took a trip there in the winter of 1974 to meet with Roger Toogood, their director. Our meeting seemed to go well and they showed a great deal of interest in the concept of the program. They had been trying to establish an overseas program to serve a long waiting list of prospective adoptive parents. I spent several days in meetings with the agency, even speaking to groups of parents registered with them. Roger suggested that he travel to Korea and visit St. Lazarus Village. He did make the trip, but he turned down our program afterwards because he felt the United States government would never allow the children to emigrate.

When I returned from Minnesota, depressed by yet another rejection, Don Scott, a charming and very visible child advocate, visited me at the office of the American-Korean Foundation. Don had heard about my search and offered to have his agency, My Friend's House, handle the program.

I checked with people in the adoption network who knew Don. The feedback was positive, and most felt that although the agency he ran was new and quite small, it was doing an effective job in Vietnam. Furthermore, it was helped by funding from the Committee of 1000, Clayton Hagen's group, which had an impeccable reputation.

I signed an agreement with My Friend's House right away. Several of their staff met with me in New York, and I then traveled to Newton, Massachusetts, to visit their office, a small room in a church building staffed by volunteers. I wasn't completely comfortable with what I found, but I was grateful to have a registered agency at last for my program.

Just when all the paperwork was completed and we were poised to proceed, Don Scott ran into difficulty with his associates and he suddenly resigned from My Friend's House. To make matters worse, while I was visiting Newton, Mac Taylor of TAISSA had telephoned Sally and Richard Darby, directors of the agency, warning them that Outreach was a "dangerous" program because the kids were at high risk for contracting and spreading leprosy. I heard the whole conversation on speaker phone:

Taylor: I think you ought to reconsider handling the Outreach program for two reasons. First, I have received *shocking* medical reports on the dangers involved, and second, these children cannot come into this country on orphan visas.

R. Darby: Mrs. Gottlieb is right here. Won't you please discuss this with her?

Taylor: What? No, I don't want to talk with her—Wayne, talk to Bernice.

Gottlieb: Wayne, what are these "shocking medical reports"?

Hinrichs: I don't know. Mac, what are these reports? (Pause) He says that the personal doctor of a WAIF board member in California is against it.

Gottlieb: Who is he? What are his qualifications?

Hinrichs: I don't know.

Gottlieb: I have sent you copies of supportive letters from leading leprologists in the world, the Center for Disease Control, and you yourselves have a positive report from HEW showing the danger to be close to zero! About the visas—we all knew they couldn't come in as orphans. Obviously! Everyone has known this from day one!

Hinrichs: We'd better have a meeting on this.

This phone call was, of course, terribly upsetting. But with Don Scott out of the picture and My Friend's House troubled by Mac Taylor's scare tactics, we terminated our agreement by mutual consent.

It had never occurred to me to seek support from a New York agency, because I didn't think any agencies except TAISSA in the New York City area were working overseas. However, I frequently spoke at adoption agencies in order to educate prospective adoptive parents about transracial adoption. One agency where I frequently spoke was Spence-Chapin Services to Families and Children, the most prestigious agency on the East Coast. At a fund-raising cocktail party that Fred and I attended in February 1975, I spoke to members of their board and their social workers about overseas adoption, the newest hot topic. Under normal circumstances, this would not have been the time or place to have a discussion about my troubles with finding an agency. But these were not exactly normal circumstances. I was pretty desperate.

The planets must all have been in alignment that day, because when I quietly broached the subject of my agency search to Jane Edwards, their director, I was taken aback by her immediate enthusiastic response. Apparently Spence-Chapin felt it was time to work with orphans from Asia and needed the contacts I had established in South Korea. Jane was supported in her decision by Rosemary Stowe, director of adoption for the agency, and eventually by the Spence-Chapin Board of Directors. Jane's first question to me was "What is our next step?" I was beside myself with joy.

Chapter 8. The Bureaucratic Nightmare: 1974

NBC aired its film about St. Lazarus and Operation Outreach on April 12 and May 27, 1974, not long after we returned from Korea. It included an interview with Dr. Rusk, the president of the American-Korean Foundation, who had been instrumental in getting the foundation involved with Outreach.

> Marjorie Margolies: Dr. Howard Rusk...is enthusiastic about the children's future, as well as the future of the program.

> Dr. Rusk: The dividends may well be more important than the principle—and that is, by demonstrating that leprosy is not an infectious, terrible, scourge type of disease. These kids will come having undergone every health regulation in the world and they're accepted as normal children, and that is as it should be.

Marjorie Margolies: What if the children do come down with the disease?

Dr. Rusk: I don't think there's one chance in a million, but if they do, so what? They'd be treated immediately and in a few months they'd be back in the community—no problem.

The *New York Times* article was published on April 12, and on April 14, the *Korea Herald* in Seoul published an article about Operation Outreach. It said that the eight children would leave for the United States in September 1974, which was what we thought and hoped at the time.

In response to both the *Times* article and the NBC report, we received literally thousands of letters expressing admiration for what we were doing. The adoptive parents who were waiting for the children had been on the show, and one of them, Janet Martino, got a telephone call on May 9 from Korea. The caller was an elderly man who did not give his name but offered congratulations on Operation Outreach. After saying what a wonderful program it was, he went on:

When I was a child, my mother had leprosy, and my father and I lived at a leper colony. Then she died, and in wondrous ways my father and I left the village to lead a life with an unknown past. I feel very fortunate because I escaped the life these poor children have and I rose to become Korean politician. I am very old now and I do not hold my position any more, but had I not escaped from the stigma itself, I too would be alone....

I have seen your Mrs. Bernice Gottlieb in our newspapers and I only wish that all heavenly blessings shower on her and her work....Her project is much talked about here and I only hope it will have an effect on the people's prejudices of leprosy patients. I pray for her and all of the new parents. She truly is—what do the Americans call it?—a pied piper, only leading the children out to freedom....

Since this adoption program has come about, I find myself, after all these many years, finally at ease with the thought of where I came from. Oh! I think I am getting to be an emotional old man.

Such responses were wonderful, of course. But I was not surprised that there were some negative responses too. Among them was a letter to *The New York Times* from Dr. Hasselblad, published on May 3, 1974. He wrote:

As president of an organization long concerned with leprosy, I must object to the kind of adoption project for children of leprosy patients described in an April 12 news story. I feel strongly that this approach is not only negative but harmful to the children and to the cause of eliminating leprosy's unjust stigma.

The separation of children from their parents and homeland for any purpose is extremely serious. And to single out leprosy as the basis for this separation only reinforces in the public mind the idea that this disease is separate from others.

Obviously his allowing me to attend the leprosy course at Carville had not changed his views of what I was trying to do. Of course, I replied, with my own letter to the *Times,* which was published on May 6.

In his letter to the *Times*...Dr. Oliver Hasselblad betrays a basic misunderstanding of the purpose of Outreach...In no way does our program imply a "feeling of hopelessness" about solving the problems connected with leprosy through research, early detection and treatment in out-patient facilities....We certainly support the work of people like Dr. Hasselblad who are attacking the medical and social problems of leprosy at ground level.

But it is a fact that the stigma against leprosy patients exists in Korea and it extends to their children. The job of eliminating the stigma will not be finished in this decade. In the meantime, the children continue to suffer. As a mother, I do appreciate Dr. Hasselblad's hesitation about separating children from their parents. But these children are not torn from their families; they are placed for adoption by parents who are destitute and many are suffering from advanced forms of the disease. It is a condition of every placement we make that the child continue to correspond with the parents back home.

Quite simply, our program is grounded in the profound belief that every single child has the right to realize his or her full potential. In Korea, at present, this is not possible for the child whose parents have leprosy. That the superstition must be eradicated goes without saying. But we cannot consider that this battle—however important or idealistic—should be fought by children.

Dr. Hasselblad believes it to be dehumanizing for a child to learn in later life that leprosy was the reason he was brought to this country. We think it infinitely worse for a child to know from early childhood that leprosy is the reason he has to live in a virtual prison in his own land.

The response to this letter was again almost entirely positive. But I knew my work was just beginning as I began exploring all possible methods of bringing the children into the States. When Fred and I had returned in March, satisfied that the Korean parents understood all the ramifications of adoption, I had proceeded to have the children's paperwork prepared to register them for emigration. Early on it had become apparent that the numerical index, or quota system, was backlogged; we were told it would take several years to bring the children to America. This was not acceptable, of course, so I explored other options.

Nancy Chasen, Margie Margolies's friend, explained how I should proceed, and I followed her instructions. I needed to contact both my local congressman and my senator and persuade them to introduce general legislation in both houses of Congress to smooth the way for these children to emigrate under "immediate relative status," bypassing the quota system. This general bill would emphasize the need for these children to be rescued from the unfair and irrational prejudice that governed their lives.

Jacob Javits was one of our senators and Hamilton Fish, Jr., was our congressman. Senator Javits's office was the most cooperative and his staff helped me in every way they possibly could. Mary McFerran and Pat Shakow, two of the senator's aides, wrote letters, made calls, and directed me to all the right people in my efforts to lobby on the children's behalf. After NBC's program, his office and ours had received more than 8000 letters of support. *The New York Times*, perhaps because its April 12 article had created so much interest, had run another article on June 4 by their reporter in Korea. It focused on the parents and their selfless reasons for giving up their children and quoted both the parents and Father Lee on their likely bleak future in Korea in contrast with their hopes for the children's life in America. This piece too generated a great deal of sympathetic response.

The publicity also generated an editorial in the *Christian Science Monitor* on June 3, part of which quoted the words of a popular song of the time:

> What the world needs now is...what it has always needed:... love, sweet love....Consider the almost Biblical sense of charity expressed in the brave new breaking of shibboleths by foster families volunteering to welcome the children of lepers from their exile in remote colonies—and into homes seeking to reflect the actual parents' expression of love in releasing their children to a better life.

After I met in Washington with Senator Javits, he agreed to ask the Immigration and Naturalization Service to "parole" the eight children into the country in time for Christmas that year (1974). A person who is not eligible to enter the country as a refugee or immigrant can be paroled into the United States by the commissioner. This method is used only for emergency, humanitarian, or public interest reasons, and Javits believed that the children would be admitted on a humanitarian basis. But of course there was no guarantee that this would happen, so I felt it was important to introduce legislation as well in case the parole option fell through.

Javits agreed to introduce the necessary legislation, which would amend the Immigration and Nationality Act so that children of parents with Hansen's disease could be classified as immediate relatives and therefore admitted without a lengthy wait. Pat Shakow, Senator Javits's aide, telephoned me on August 14 to say they had started to draft a general legislation bill that would basically create a new definition of an adoptable child—one whose parents are victims of a disease such as leprosy and who would enter the United States under the auspices of a recognized child placement agency approved by the secretary of state. I also heard from Senator Lowell Weicker of Connecticut, who had been very sympathetic to the program. He said he expected to hear something "fairly soon" from the State Department about the children's parole, and that Senator Javits had been in touch with him about helping with the legislation. The Senate bill, S.3995, was introduced on September 12 by Senator Javits.

Then Pat Tassio, an aide to Representative Fish, called to say that Fish would like to meet with me on his next visit to New York on September 4. It took me an hour to reach the regional office in Peekskill, and I waited another two hours in the crowded, cramped space. Every time the door opened and someone went in or out, I could see Representative Fish at his desk in the smoke-filled, windowless office. Outside in the reception area, aides busily scurried about, greeting the continuous flow of constituents seeking favors of one kind or another.

When my turn finally came, I was greeted by the congressman, who was dabbing at his reddened eyes with a limp handkerchief. I introduced myself, and he skimmed the various documents I presented. These included letters of support from prominent doctors and personal pleas for help from the adoptive parents.

"But why do you want to bring these lepers' children here?" he asked, genuinely puzzled and seeming to have difficulty focusing on the conversation. I knew I had only a few minutes to convince him and I tried to be as concise as possible. I explained that Senator Javits was introducing a bill in the Senate, co-sponsored by Senator Weicker, and that we needed a companion bill in the House of Representatives. I hoped that he would be willing to introduce this bill for us and that he would also introduce private bills to permit adoptions by the four adoptive families, in case the general bill did not pass.

"Why me?" he whined. I told him that a number of his constituents were involved in the program and showed him a petition from local families. What I didn't say was that I needed him because a) he was a Republican and b) he was a member of the House Sub-Committee on Immigration, Citizenship and International Law. Javits's aides thought it would be a big help if Fish were involved.

After a silence, he said he would look into the matter and make his decision after contacting the Center for Disease Control for clearance. I mumbled a rather feeble goodbye, feeling I hadn't reached him. His eyes were bothering him and he was terribly uncomfortable. On the way out, I stopped at a drugstore across the street from his office and bought some Visine eye drops. I went back, past an imperious aide, and walked right into the congressman's office. I handed him the eye drops and left without waiting for a reply, feeling all was lost anyway so far as he was concerned. However, to my surprise and delight, Representative Fish introduced the companion bill, H.R.16737, in the House of Representatives on September 19; he also introduced the four private bills (H.R. 1394, 1395, 1396, and 1397) on October 2.

Meanwhile, Leonard Chapman, Commissioner of the Immigration and Naturalization Service, was considering the request from Senator Javits to "parole" the eight children into the country in time for Christmas 1974.

On October 23, a newspaper in Newburgh, New York, was one of many papers to publish a syndicated article from the *Los Angeles Times* about Operation Outreach. It began:

On one side of the world in a leprosy village in South Korea, two healthy sisters, Mee-Kyung Cho, 3, and Hee-Kyung Cho, 1, wait, sentenced by their society to a bleak future because of the disease of their father.

93o CONGRESS
2D SESSION **H. R. 16737**

IN THE HOUSE OF REPRESENTATIVES

SEPTEMBER 19, 1974

Mr. FISH introduced the following bill; which was referred to the Committee on the Judiciary

A BILL

To amend the Immigration and Nationality Act to provide for the immigration of children of individuals suffering from Hansen's disease.

1   *Be it enacted by the Senate and House of Representa-*
2 *tives of the United States of America in Congress assembled,*
3 That (a) section 101 (b) (1) of the Immigration and
4 Nationality Act is amended—

5   (1) by striking out the period at the end of sub-
6   paragraph (F) and inserting in lieu thereof a semicolon
7   and "or"; and

8   (2) by adding after subparagraph (F) the follow-
9   ing new subparagraph:

10   "(G) a child, under the age of fourteen at the time

I

The general bill, H.R. 16737, introduced in the House by Representative Hamilton Fish, Jr., in September 1974.

And 7,000 miles away, Janet and Louis Martino, a New York City policeman and his wife with two youngsters of their own, also wait, eager to offer the two Asian children a fresh chance in America.

By January, if some tangled immigration problems are overcome, the two children—part of an initial group of eight—will inaugurate an unusual overseas adoption plan believed to be the first of its kind. An area congressman, Rep. Hamilton Fish Jr., Millbrook Republican, wants to ease these obstacles.

The article went on to talk about my meeting Father Lee and deciding to start Outreach, the government obstacles that stood in the way, the facts about Hansen's disease itself, and the terrible stigma that blighted the lives of both the parents who had Hansen's disease and their children who did not. A photograph of me and Susannah, then seven, accompanied this "human interest" piece. It ended with a quote from a letter that Mr. Cho had sent to the Martinos that month. "It is very sad to have our children leave us. But we feel happy knowing they will be loved, in good health, and will have a good education." Articles like this helped generate support for Outreach, which was important as we waited for the government to take action.

At this critical time, when we believed that Chapman was about to take positive action on our behalf, Mary McFerran, Javits's aide, called me to say we had run into a serious problem. The State Department had received information that the eight children were being separated from their natural parents by force; the department was planning to investigate this charge and others that had been made by a reputable organization. Mary suggested that we reword the parental release documents in order to clarify the situation.

When I asked Mary who had made these outrageous charges against us, she said she couldn't tell me because it was classified information. I then called Hamilton Fish's aide, Jessica, who had already heard the news. She too said the information was classified. I wondered how classified, how important to United States security could information on eight children be? Jessica said there was nothing we could do now except to get the documents of proof into both Javits's and Fish's hands as soon as possible.

I placed a call to Korea and spoke with Youn Taek Tahk, director of our cooperating Korean agency, Social Welfare Society. Mr. Tahk was shocked at the accusation. He had personally interviewed the parents several times and knew how anxious they were to place the children with American families.

Mr. Tahk devised a new parental release document, however, and then took all the parents before a judge in a Seoul court to stamp and verify their signatures once again. These documents arrived a week later and I took them to Washington myself. It had all been very costly, emotionally and financially.

Then, in November, Mary McFerran called me. "Bernice," she said sadly, "our request for parole has been denied. This accusation killed it."

We had been so close. Most of the adoptive parents had already purchased Christmas presents for the children (which they now quickly sent to Korea). Now we would have to start all over again. As 1974 drew to a close and President Ford prepared to set off on a trip to Korea, I sent a telegram to Mrs. Ford, begging her "as one mother to another" to ask her husband to grant entry visas for the children. I never received an answer. John and Fran Daley on December 1 sent a letter to the president. In very moving words, they explained that they had been waiting for their children for more than a year and they were turning to him because they had no one else to turn to. But all of this did no good.

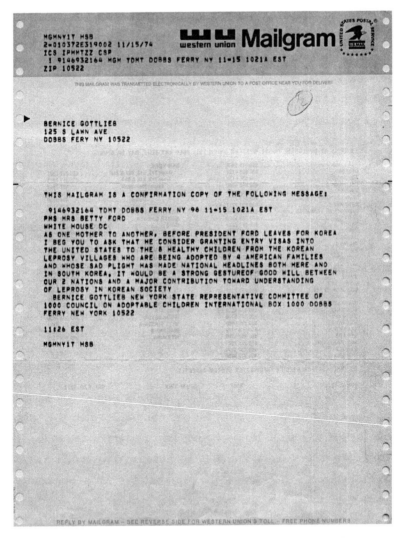

The telegram Bernice sent to Betty Ford asking for her help.

Late in December, the Edwardses received a touching letter from Korea dated December 13.

Dear my Foster Parents,

It is snow-falling winter now. Thank you for the card and the money you kindly sent to me. My parents are also very grateful to you.

We had snow-falls here, and I wonder how it may be there.

We have been in vacation since December 11th to last for 50 days.

It will be Christmas very soon. We hear Mass at twelve midnight on the 24th. 1974 is passing away and 1975 is coming. I pray that your intentions may be fulfilled in 1975. Please be careful not to catch cold, and have a good Christmas and a Happy New Year.

Ae Sook Song

There was also the matter of clearing up the charges that were now in the State Department's files. I telephoned the Government Operations Committee in Washington and made an appointment to see their counsel, James Kronfeld. I requested information on the charges against me under the Freedom of Information Act. He told me that the type of classification put on this information meant it could only be related to me by the authors of my bills. However, he cautioned, they might have reasons for not sharing this information with me. It was up to me, he said, to demand this information from them.

I knew I couldn't do that—these were the only people in the government who had understood Operation Outreach and who had actually done anything to help it succeed. But eventually, through someone who worked at the Korean desk of the State Department, I learned that a powerful organization called World Vision had accused me of planning to "steal the children from their parents and sell them in the United States."

World Vision is a Christian relief and development organization that works in many poor countries. One of their interests was working in leprosy resettlement villages, and they apparently felt we were infringing on their territory.

I learned later that Harriet Wood, one of the officers of World Vision of Korea, had written to the American-Korean Foundation in June, apparently after reading an article about Outreach in a Korean newspaper. Dorothy Irvine, Executive Director of the Foundation, wrote back to her:

Dear Mrs. Wood:

...News stories, because of their brevity, cannot tell a complete story and often lead to misunderstanding. We can assure you, however, that our adoption program in no way implies "the purposeful breakup of family relationships in order to provide children for adoption." This program grew out of the concern of a number of families at St. Lazarus Village who were determined to seek a better life for their children....

...The parents who apply to us for assistance must meet certain requirements and will be counseled so that they fully understand the ramifications of permanent adoption before they are considered eligible for this program.

...It is required that family ties be continued through correspondence and photographs in an unusual sharing of love between the two families and at maturity, if the child so desires, he may return to his homeland. Outreach differs, in this important way, from all other existing adoption programs. It is basically a service provided to individual families in resettlement villages who seek help which is presently unavailable to them.

...We certainly support the work of organizations such as yours who are attacking the medical and social problems of leprosy at ground level. But it is a fact that there is still a great deal of work needed to eradicate the stigma, ignorance and fear which extends to the children of leprosy patients.

The American-Korean Foundation...hopes to realize fully the goals of the Outreach program.

Dorothy Irvine no doubt expected that her letter would resolve any issues that World Vision was concerned about. But almost six months later, the problem had not been completely eradicated.

Also, there was enormous resistance to Operation Outreach in many parts of the government. Because of the sensationalism that the term "leprosy" evokes, there was a lot of communication between Washington and the medical community. Fortunately the CDC remained steadfast, an important and knowledgeable ally. There were many other medical allies and, interestingly, very few negative reactions from the general public. All I wanted to do was bring eight children to the United States. So many orphans and other immigrants had come in with very little attention—many of them with unreported diseases of various kinds. Our children had been examined thoroughly and found to be extremely healthy and well-cared-for. How to convince Congress of this!

The obsession I had developed kept my adrenaline going all the time. Through all the obstacles and disappointments, I maintained a high level of hope. There was no way I would give up: I would do what it took to bring the children here.

I was amazed at how money to support Outreach kept coming in. I never had to write a grant proposal; the minute I needed money, someone would pop out of the woodwork and offer some. From my first grant through Dr. Rusk until my work was completed, I was fortunate and truly appreciative for this financial assistance.

After our terrible disappointment when parole was denied and we learned the children would not be here for Christmas after all, we explored all possibilities, whether legal or not so legal. Our final plan, and we were completely serious about it, was to ask Father Lee to obtain Canadian visas for the children as if they were all going on a vacation. Then I would drive to Canada, meet them at a designated place, and drive the children over the border to the United States. I had previously taken Susannah to Canada and back, and no one at the border had questioned her citizenship. I thought of asking some Asian friends to accompany us, to look as if they were the children's parents, but then I realized they would be in legal jeopardy if I were to be arrested.

I telephoned my friend Julie Harris (the actress, who then lived near us and who had been very supportive of Outreach). "What if," I said to her, "the children were flown into Canada and the adoptive parents each brought two of the children across the border?" I knew there was a strong possibility that the authorities might stop us, but there was also a chance that we could cross. Whether they stopped us or not, I felt we could garner tremendous public sympathy and support. I asked Julie what she thought, and she said she would wait on the American side of the border to show her support for what we were doing, and she would make a public appeal on our behalf if necessary. I then called Margie Margolies, who agreed to have NBC News waiting at the border as well.

Armed with this new scheme, I called a meeting of the parents. Arlene couldn't make it but said she would go along with whatever we did. Slightly crazy by this time from all the work we had done, we all decided to try the Canadian route.

Fred walked into our meeting after a long day in the city and immediately put a stop to our proposed action. "First of all," he said, "you should all calm down and remember why you are bringing these children in. It is to show the Korean people that the U.S. welcomes them, despite their circumstances. If you bring them in illegally, the message is lost and negative and will have no impact at all."

Of course, he was right.

**Bernice and Julie Harris at a fundraiser party for Outreach:
Julie had just made an eloquent speech and then introduced Bernice.**

Just after Christmas, at the end of 1974, I received a letter from Dr. Merlin Brubaker, whose title was Regional Advisor on Leprosy and Venereal Disease for the Pan American Health Organization, part of the World Health Organization; it expressed great interest in and complete support for the Outreach program. I sent copies of his letter to Senators Javits and Weicker, Representative Fish, and everyone else I could think of. In my cover letter to Alexander Cook, counsel to the House Judiciary Committee, I said that we were anxiously awaiting the return of Congress after the holidays and the outcome of the private bills that had been introduced by Hamilton Fish (by then the private bills seemed to be our best hope). I went on, "We are fearful that [the eight children's] long wait of one and a half years is damaging both the children and their natural parents....I am most anxious to see them here in the United States and so are officials of the Republic of Korea who feel that the heavy media coverage given this program in Korea will be counterproductive to the leprosy cause in their country if the children do not arrive soon."

Chapter 9. The Struggle: 1975

In January 1975, Alexander Cook called to suggest more names for me to contact. He thought I should write a personal plea to Joshua Eilberg, chairman of the Subcommittee on Immigration, Citizenship and International Law of the House Judiciary Committee, about the children's long-drawn-out wait, and he also suggested that I call the assistant to the Judiciary Committee's chief counsel to ask about the status of the legislation.

The beginning of the year saw the convening of the 94th Congress, and on January 14, Hamilton Fish re-introduced the four private bills (H.R. 1394, 1395, 1396, and 1397) that would permit the adoptions by the four families. An article in the White Plains *Reporter Dispatch*, headlined "Fish reintroduces proposal for Korean-American reunions," described the difficulties Outreach had been encountering and said "Louis and Janet Martino... and three other families participating in the national 'Operation Outreach' adoption program, have been caught for months in a web of bureaucracy that prevents the children's immediate entry into this country." On

January 30, Senator Javits re-introduced the bill (now S. 494) that he had introduced the previous September. Like Fish's bills, which had been referred to the House Judiciary Committee, Javits's was referred to the Senate Judiciary Committee. Attached to the bill and printed in the Congressional Record was Outreach's statement of purpose, which described the stigma and misunderstanding that surrounded the idea of leprosy and provided information about the disease and the adoption plans for the eight children.

I continued to travel to Washington, D.C., to meet with the Immigration, Citizenship and International Law Subcommittee members and anyone else who might be helpful to us, and I sent information packets and spoke on the telephone to people in the White House, the Congress, and all the involved government departments.

All this time, the prospective adoptive parents continued to call me at least once a week—some of them felt I wasn't doing enough to move things forward, and there was a lot of emotion floating back and forth. And of course I was in touch with them whenever I had any news at all or when I received a letter from the parents at St. Lazarus, translated into English by one of the Carmelite nuns. This didn't happen very frequently, and I don't know if that made the waiting harder or easier for the anxious adoptive parents in the United States.

On March 5, I learned that even though I had earlier been given the "privileged" information that World Vision had been the source of the misinformation about Outreach, the State Department had just received "classified" information about our case, and therefore the hearing scheduled for that day on the four private bills before the House Immigration Subcommittee had been postponed. I immediately wrote to James Kronfeld, with whom I had earlier been in touch about the accusations against Outreach, and explained that although all the previous accusations had been cleared up to everyone's satisfaction, it seemed that new ones had been lodged. I asked for his help in getting the whole thing resolved once and for all.

Congressional Record

United States of America

PROCEEDINGS AND DEBATES OF THE 94th CONGRESS, FIRST SESSION

Vol. 121   WASHINGTON, THURSDAY, JANUARY 30, 1975   **No. 11**

Senate

By Mr. JAVITS:
S. 494. A bill to amend the Immigration and Nationality Act to provide for the immigration of children of individuals suffering from Hansen's disease. Referred to the Committee on the Judiciary.

OPERATION OUTREACH

Mr. JAVITS. Mr. President, a sad situation in the Republic of Korea has been brought to the attention of a group of New Yorkers who have taken steps to provide new opportunities for a group of children. Specifically, they are the children of persons who are suffering from Hansen's disease—although they do not have the disease themselves—and as such are required to live in "leprosy villages" in Korea. While the Public Health Service assures us that these children do not themselves suffer from Hansen's disease, all opportunity for a normal life for the children is cut off as soon as their parent's affliction becomes known.

New Yorkers associated with Operation Outreach, working with the American-Korean Foundation and International Social Service have arranged for some of the children to be adopted by American families, and the Korean parents have given their consent to the adoptions, knowing that life in this country will provide a better life for their children. But, there is a roadblock in the form of the immigration laws of the United States which prohibit the entry of these children into this country for adoption by American citizens if the parents of the children are themselves living. My bill seeks to remove the impediment in this one particular case.

Mr. President, I ask unanimous consent that material explaining this program be printed at this point in the RECORD, and I send the bill to the desk for appropriate reference.

There being no objection, the material was ordered to be printed in the RECORD, as follows:

OUTREACH: STATEMENT OF PURPOSE

INTRODUCTION

It has been said that "prejudice is the child of ignorance." The truth of that statement has been demonstrated for centuries in the case of leprosy, a mildly contagious and easily arrested disease which nevertheless sentences its victims and their children to the severest kind of human suffering, degradation and discrimination. The prejudice

against those who have leprosy has survived since Biblical times, and the fear of leprosy persists even though modern medical science now understands and can arrest and control the disease. (So strong is this prejudice that the dictionary defines the word leper as: "a person shunned for moral and social reasons.")

Today we know that a germ, and not a cure or a demon causes leprosy. (The leprosy bacteria was first described by Dr. Gerhard A. Hansen in 1874 and leprosy is medically known as Hansen's Disease.) Leprosy is a disease which attacks the nerves and eventually robs its victims of the important warning signal of pain. In its late stages leprosy can sometimes so deaden sensation that people who have the disease wear down their fingers and toes through use. Leprosy can also produce severe deformities. The affects have given rise to the myth that leprosy eats away tissues and causes toes and fingers to "drop off." The truth is that all of the major complications of leprosy are preventable, and the disease can be arrested through prompt treatment.

Leprosy is one of the world's least contagious diseases—much less virulent than tuberculosis for instance. Nurses and doctors who work with leprosy patients rarely contract the disease. In fact, in the 75 years of its existence, not a single staff member of the United States Public Health Service Hospital in Carville, Louisiana, which handles leprosy patients, has contracted leprosy. Research has shown that only five percent of the world's population is susceptible to leprosy bacillus and even that five percent will only contract the disease after prolonged and close contact with an infected person. No evidence has ever been found that the disease is inherited.

But the stigma that is attached to leprosy causes many of its victims to hide their affliction until it is too late since treatment in many countries—including the Republic of Korea—means isolation for them and for their families in squalid leprosoria or resettlement villages. Those with leprosy and those whose parents have leprosy are considered second class citizens and are cut off forever from equal opportunities in all areas of their lives: employment, education and even marriage. Segregation from uninfected villages makes prolonged contact with leprosy patients unavoidable for uninfected family members forced to live there, and a number of them may contract the disease needlessly because of being coerced into this isolation.

It can truly be said that the fear and loathing which society maintains towards those with leprosy is more dangerous and damaging and disfiguring than the leprosy bacillus itself.

The program described in the following pages aims at doing something about the intolerable conditions in which people with leprosy and their families are forced to live.

OUTREACH, a program of the American-Korean Foundation, seeks to bring children of leprosy patients to the United States for adoption. Every one of these children will be arranged in Korea and will be medically followed here in the United States to insure that there is not the slightest chance that they have leprosy. By removing them from a society which discriminates against them, the individual child will benefit. In addition, the health and well-being of these children and their accomplishments in an atmosphere free of prejudice will demonstrate that the stigma against leprosy can be erased.

This is a radical, efficient and humane solution to a centuries-old problem which is causing thousands of children to suffer and denies them the realization of their full potential.

BACKGROUND

Leprosy affects in excess of 15 million of the world's people. While it is not limited to any race or geographic distribution, the greatest number of cases occur in the tropical or semi-tropical climates of Africa, Southeast Asia, South America, and the Indian continent.

In the United States the incidence is limited to approximately 3,000 cases, the majority, of which receive outpatient treatment. Leprosy is not native to the United States and health officials say there is no documentation of a second generation of the disease in this country.

We do not know how many Koreans have leprosy which they are hiding, but some 90 resettlement villages house 25,000 known leprosy and ex-leprosy patients and thousands who are socially branded because a relative was found to have the disease.

Children of leprosy victims are able to leave the village at maturity, so long as they are free of the disease. However, the name of the leprosy village is permanently imprinted on their papers so that potential employers and the police will be able to identify them. They are forced to take the most menial of jobs and are prevented from attending Korean schools. The stigma of leprosy often extends even to marriage and restricts the possibilities of choosing a mate.

THE NEED

The Korean Ministry of Health and Social Affairs places the number of uninfected children living in leprosy villages at about 7,000. Unless a way is found to erode the leprosy barrier and free these healthy children from these villages, they will grow up bearing the stigma of leprosy and will live out their lives as second class citizens. The fear and prejudice in Korea has created a climate in which they not only have virtually no hope for a normal life.

＊ ＊ ＊

more....

The general legislation introduced in the Senate by Senator Jacob Javits and recorded in the Congressional Record of January 30, 1975.

94rit CONGRESS
1st Session

S. 494

IN THE SENATE OF THE UNITED STATES

JANUARY 30, 1975

Mr. JAVITS introduced the following bill; which was read twice and referred to the Committee on the Judiciary

A BILL

To amend the Immigration and Nationality Act to provide for the immigration of children of individuals suffering from Hansen's disease.

1 *Be it enacted by the Senate and House of Representa-*
2 *tives of the United States of America in Congress assembled,*
3 That (a) section 101 (b) (1) of the Immigration and Na-
4 tionality Act is amended—
5   (1) by striking out the period at the end of sub-
6   paragraph (F) and inserting in lieu thereof a semicolon
7   and "or"; and
8   (2) by adding after subparagraph (F) the follow-
9   ing new subparagraph:

II

In the meantime, the House Judiciary Committee was waiting for reports from various departments before beginning to consider Hamilton Fish's bill to amend the Immigration and Nationality Act. Senator Javits, feeling that the general legislation was stalled and going nowhere, wrote to our ambassador to Korea, Richard Sneider, asking for his help in expediting the children's admission to the United States by means of a parole issued by the attorney general.

There were lots of gloomy days. Sometimes, when one of the adoptive parents called and started crying, I was upset for the rest of the day. Janet Martino used to react to her frustrations by getting really angry at the Establishment. She would say, "Bernice, you're so damn naive; you believe all the crap they're handing you. Don't you realize they're just humoring us! Don't you understand they don't ever intend to let the kids in!"

Betty Edwards, the dearest, most marvelous person, starting crying one day when I talked to her. Who would have thought that sturdy, dependable Betty would ever break down? John Daley telephoned for status reports every three or four days; I began to dread his calls because I never had anything to tell him. John also checked Washington monthly, calling the visa division of the State Department to see if the non-preference quota, by some miracle, had opened up. Our kids had been registered in July and August of 1974, and their coming in strictly on the numerical index from Asia had always been possible. However, the Vietnam influx in April 1975, when Vietnam fell, set the quota back on its heels and kept it tightly closed.

That month I learned that the Immigration Subcommittee was waiting for questions to be answered by State Department officials in Korea and that the president would not intervene in the nonpreference visa process, meaning that the children would have to wait their turn. In May I wrote to Ambassador Sneider; I said that the nonpreference quota now appeared out of our reach and asked his help in obtaining paroles from the attorney general or the commissioner of immigration.

His reply was discouraging; he said the embassy had submitted the required reports in April, that they would "take prompt final action" when the private bills were passed or the children's numbers came up, but otherwise their hands were tied.

Sometimes the pressure from the waiting adoptive parents was unbearable. I suffered for each of them and for all of them, and for the families in Korea and the eight waiting children. All through the years, however, I managed to put on a cheerful face and encouraged the families to be proactive, to write, gather petitions, make speeches, lobby, or do whatever they felt would help. I needed all the help I could get, but at the end of the day I knew it was really my own battle.

There was never a moment when I admitted defeat either to myself or to anyone involved. In spite of the terrible odds against us, I always believed the children would come because I knew that I would stop at nothing to bring them here.

I became a thorn in the side of anyone involved with immigration, from the people in the New York section of the Immigration and Naturalization Service to all of the departments in Washington. State, Justice, and Health, Education and Welfare all got involved in this cause, as did the attorney general, the commissioner of immigration, and the counsel to the president in the White House. I was unrelenting. I badgered, cajoled, made promises, anything that might move the big bureaucracy into action.

I was filled with a deep sense of responsibility for what I had started. I began to feel that I was one of the children, that I was the parent with leprosy, that I was the anxious adoptive parent filled with anguish at the difficulties we were enduring. And I was. I was all these people and I suffered terribly. It was the first time in my life that I prayed so fervently, and that was my only comfort.

In June, Senator Javits wrote again to Attorney General Edward Levi, explaining that the children's quota numbers would not be reached in the foreseeable future and therefore he was asking Levi to consider his request for parole again. But by September, he had received no reply from Levi.

Even things that were fun sometimes had an edge. Fred and I had a party in August to celebrate the engagement of Marjorie Margolies, NBC-TV news reporter and single mother of two adopted Asian girls, and Edward Mezvinsky, congressman from Iowa. Margie had met Ed when she did a news special about the most eligible bachelors on Capitol Hill. It was love at first sight, and they were in New York when Ed popped the question, so they had come to Dobbs Ferry to share the good news with us. The first thing Ed did when he met us was to ask what he could do to help me in Washington. These two extraordinary people, first Margie and then Ed, had come into my life like some kind of miracle. I couldn't believe my good fortune. Now some seventy or eighty guests at our house on Southlawn Avenue were celebrating their engagement.

One of Ed's invited guests was Hamilton Fish, Jr. I was standing in the group around Representative and Mrs. Fish when she said, "I am really concerned about Ham's re-election. He is co-sponsoring an outlandish bill to bring lepers into this country!"

Marjorie Margolies and Representative Ed Mezvinsky
after announcing their engagement.

In the morning on October 5, the day of Margie and Ed's wedding in Maryland, the two brothers of Margie's daughter Lee Heh arrived from Korea. I had found a wonderful family to adopt them, but even before taking them to meet their new family, we piled them into our car at the airport and drove them to the wedding, reuniting them with their long-lost sister. One of the other guests was Garner Cline, who was staff director of the House Judiciary Committee as well as counsel to the Subcommittee on Immigration, Citizenship, and International Law. At the reception, he said to Fred, "The CIA and the FBI both looked into your wife's background—we know more about her than you do!" Fred and I just looked at each other and didn't think much about his comment. But I was later told by some of the legislative aides I dealt with that I had been very thoroughly checked out.

Ed's assistant had called me in July to ask for various pieces of information, and Ed continued to try to move our Outreach program forward. I was busy gathering recommendations from prominent scientists and doctors to send to the members of the Subcommittee on Immigration. For example, after much correspondence with me, Dr. Albert Solnit, a professor of pediatrics and psychiatry at Yale Medical School and director of Yale's Child Study Center, sent a letter to Congressman Eilberg, which urged Eilberg to support passage of the private bills and went on:

> As you know, the decision to place these children in adoption was made two years ago by the natural parents who live in a Leprosy village in Korea. Their judgment is that their children will have a better life if they can be adopted and brought up in the United States. Since this procedure has already been started, I want to urge that it be brought to as swift and decisive a conclusion as possible since children cannot tolerate such passage of time without great risk to their development.

At the beginning of August 1975, Hamilton Fish called to apologize for the subcommittee's failure to get to the private bills before the summer recess. He said they would consider them as soon as the members returned in September. Meanwhile, he asked me for another "statement of purpose," which would emphasize the primary purpose of informing the public, with adoption as secondary.

At last, on September 11, the Subcommittee on Immigration, Citizenship, and International Law began to hear testimony about the four private bills. The members of the subcommittee were Joshua Eilberg, Democrat of Pennsylvania (Chairman); Paul Sarbanes, Democrat of Maryland; Elizabeth Holtzman, Democrat of New York; Chris Dodd, Democrat of Connecticut; Marty Russo, Democrat of Illinois; William Cohen, Republican of Maine; and of course, Hamilton Fish, Jr., Republican of New York. I had visited all of them regularly.

Before the hearing, I went to Fish's office and met with him and Ed Mezvinsky as well as Fish's assistant Jessica Goldstein and Alexander Cook, the subcommittee's associate counsel. They asked me two questions: first, how would we guarantee the five-year medical check-ups for the children? I said Spence-Chapin would take care of that. Second, did I plan to pursue additional private legislation after these bills were enacted? I said I did.

Then we went to the hearing room and Congressman Fish introduced me to the chairman, Representative Eilberg, who said he was impressed with my work with Outreach and was in favor of the private bills. His manner was very warm and kind; he took my hand in both of his and told me he knew that I had worked so hard for the parents and the children. I was very touched. When the hearing began, Ed Mezvinsky spoke eloquently about the children and parents and about the medical evidence that showed the invisibly small risk of the children being infected. Then Fish presented information about Spence-Chapin's involvement, the Public Health Service's views about the lack of any danger of infection, and all the careful research and hard work Outreach had done. The subcommittee's vote was unanimous in favor, and the bills were referred to the Judiciary Committee. Hooray, I thought, we're one step closer!

Afterward I met with Alexander Cook about what information he would need for the Judiciary Committee. This was our first meeting in person, and I was pleased to see that he got very interested in what Outreach was doing. He also wanted some further documents about the medical follow-ups and the children's medical forms, which I sent to him as soon as I got home. But a couple of days later he called in an agitated state, shouting that the private bills were in jeopardy. He said that Jessica Goldstein from Representative Fish's office was also on the phone and they both had questions for me.

Al accused me of lying about the plans for medical follow-up for the children. He had telephoned Jane Edwards at Spence-Chapin, and she had denied that Spence-Chapin was going to handle the follow-up for the first eight children. He told me that this part of the plan was attached to the private bills and had already been submitted to the subcommittee, and he demanded an explanation from me.

I was quite surprised, but I explained to both of them that TAISSA had originally been involved and they had later dropped out. I said that since Spence-Chapin had taken it over, it seemed only logical that they should also handle the first eight children. But I had not discussed this with Spence-Chapin yet; in my defense, I didn't know that the private bills specified which agency would do the follow-up. Al repeated that he had just finished speaking with Jane Edwards and she was not aware that I wanted her to take on the medical responsibility for the eight kids, but Congressman Fish had put into the record that Spence was doing this. Al was livid, and so was Jessica.

I still couldn't understand what all the fuss was about. I apologized, saying that I hadn't known the particular agency was important as long as it was being done. I had assumed it would be confusing to have two agencies listed in the record as handling the program. Al was beyond reason, however, screaming at me that I had made a terrible and serious mistake.

I asked what I could do to straighten things out. He said that each agency that had done the home studies for the adoptive parents should give us a written promise that they would handle the medical follow-up. I told him this was impossible, because their normal responsibility covered only the six-month post-adoption period. I said that instead, with his permission, I would contact Spence-Chapin again and ask them to take care of this matter. He shouted, "They will never do it, I know they won't!" and slammed down the phone.

I called Jane immediately. Without any fuss at all, she agreed to take responsibility for the follow-ups; in fact, she welcomed it as the logical thing to do. I called Al right back to tell him. He was surprised that it had all been so simple to clear up—he sounded as worn out as I felt.

Jane mailed her letter to Al immediately. A few days later, when Rosemary Stowe of Spence-Chapin telephoned Al to ask what the agency could do to assist the legislation, aside from the medical follow-up, he said, "You can help change the abortion laws so people can adopt American babies! So they won't bring garbage into this country!"

Soon afterward, I called him and tried to make him understand how hard it was for someone with no legislative experience to deal with the bureaucratic obstacles and complexities we had encountered. He told me that I had asked for my difficulties by coming up with such an outlandish program and that now all these obstacles were being dumped in his lap. "They will come to this country and they will infect our schoolchildren," he said, "and Congressman Fish will be held responsible!"

In September, Peter and Betty Edwards went to Korea; they wrote to me about their experience:

September 17th – Our Great Day

Dear Bernice and Fred,

We really can't begin to tell you all of what we have been doing since we left the States. We have been so overwhelmed at things we have seen and done...

We were picked up at 9:30 this morning in Father Lee's car.... Directly we got [to St. Lazarus Village], both of the girls were standing there waiting for us. Words cannot describe how Peter and I felt when we first saw them. They immediately took to us as if we had known them all our lives. They held our hands and took us all around the village, we had so much fun together. We had a Korean-English book so were able to communicate a little. They were laughing as we were describing things, but they are very bright and understood us. They loved the gifts we gave them.

We met Ae Sook's mother and Mi Yun's father, and they were smiling at us as if they were happy and pleased with us. We had lunch with Father Lee and guests.

Tell Janet her two girls are lovely. They liked their gifts. We also saw Arlene's girls and took photographs of them. We have yet to meet Fran and John's children. We stayed for about three hours. The girls kept saying to people in the village "Mother and Father," so they really have accepted us, Bernice, and we are so overjoyed with them.

...NBC have been chasing us since we left Tokyo and we have just had a phone call from them. They are flying over from Tokyo and will be picking us up at our hotel and coming with us to the village for filming on Friday morning.

We really have had a wonderful day and thank God for giving us two lovely daughters.

God Bless,
All our love,

Betty and Peter

The NBC piece was aired on October 1 on the 7:00 PM news:

And now, this evening a story from Korea about some children who are caught in an unusual trap, and about two Americans who want to do something about it. Don Oliver reports:

Mr. and Mrs. Peter Edwards traveled 8,000 miles from their home in Long Island to this Korean village just to see two children, two Korean children they have been trying for three years to adopt. There are eight children in this village waiting to be adopted by Americans and taken off to the United States.

The Edwardses brought gifts for all of them. This is not a normal adoptive situation. Each of the children has two living parents, but their parents are lepers. This is a leper village. They are forced to live here isolated from the rest of

Korean society. It does not matter that the parents' disease can't be communicated. They must stay here. These children in this village are just as healthy and normal as any kids anywhere, but they are the children of lepers. They will carry that stigma with them wherever they go in this country.

The leprosy victims in St. Lazarus Village were told that some American families were willing to adopt their children. It was not an easy decision, but the Korean parents say they volunteered to give up their children so they could escape the poverty and stigma of living in a leper village.

There have been charges made that the parents were coerced into giving up their children or that somebody was making money out of the adoptions. The Edwardses deny the charges.

Peter Edwards: "It's pretty obvious. We have three Korean children already, and we certainly didn't buy them and we're not buying these. In fact, they cost quite a little bit of money, but I think that there was some argument about whether they should be taken away from their parents, but the children absolutely have no hope of any life at all unless they leave this village. They'll always have the stigma of leprosy on them."

Don Oliver: "If they remain in Korea?"

Peter Edwards: "If they remain in Korea, yes."

The adoptions were supposed to have gone through in September of last year, but they were held up. The evacuation of Vietnamese refugees interfered. There were so many Vietnamese entering the United States that the American government closed the quota for all other Asians.

The Edwardses plan to spend a week with the Korean children in St. Lazarus Village. Then they plan to return to Long Island and begin lobbying for a bill now before Congress which would allow these children of lepers special permission to enter the United States.

Some of the statements in the NBC report were not entirely correct, but again, there was a tremendous and sympathetic response to it.

In October the private bills were approved by the Judiciary Committee, and they were passed by the House of Representatives on November 17. I sent a telegram to Father Lee at St. Lazarus: "Bills today passed House of Representatives Senate next step Thank God." The first stop in the Senate was the Judiciary Committee, and Senator Javits wrote to its chairman, Senator Eastland, to ask that the bills be considered.

But on December 4, Ed Mezvinsky's aide called. It seemed that Senator Eastland was angry with the House Judiciary Committee because their mainly Democratic members had been giving him a hard time on some private bills he wanted passed. Therefore, it would be better politically to work only through the Republican Hamilton Fish on the House committee; he would get in touch with the two Republican senators from New York, Javits and Buckley. I was learning a lot about how our government really works.

94TH CONGRESS } HOUSE OF REPRESENTATIVES { REPORT
1st Session }   { No. 94-584

MEE KYUNG CHO AND HEE KYUNG CHO

OCTOBER 28, 1975.—Committed to the Committee of the Whole House and
ordered to be printed

Mr. EILBERG, from the Committee on the Judiciary,
submitted the following

REPORT

[To accompany H.R. 1395]

The Committee on the Judiciary, to whom was referred the bill
(H.R. 1395), for the relief of Mee Kyung Cho and Hee Kyung Cho,
having considered the same, report favorably thereon with amendments and recommend that the bill as amended do pass.

The amendments are as follows:

On page 1, line 6, after the word "Act," strike out the word "and"
and insert in lieu thereof the language "upon approval of".

On page 1, line 8, after "United States," strike our "may be approved".

On page 1, line 10, after the words "of the" strike out the word
"beneficiary" and substitute the word "beneficiaries".

PURPOSE OF THE BILL

The purpose of this bill, as amended, is to facilitate admission into
the United States of two prospective adoptive children of adoptive
parents who are citizens of the United States. The amendments are
technical in nature and the bill has been amended in accordance with
established precedents.

GENERAL INFORMATION

Beneficiaries reside in Korea with their natural parents in St.
Lazarus Village, Korea, which is a community established for lepers.
The natural father is the only family member afflicted with the disease.
Beneficiaries are coming to the United States for adoption by U.S.
citizens, ages 31 and 25, who have a daughter and son, ages 4 and 1½.
The Beneficiaries are sisters, ages 4 and 2, natives and citizens of
Korea. A home study was conducted by an approved adoption service
with a favorable recommendation.

57-007

One of the reports for the four private bills, October 1975.

RC/I Global Telegram

ZCZC   LTB9999   TJI 0345   - 26

Dest. Ind. ──────── CO.   914 6932164

TDN DOBBSFERRYNY

Confirmation Copy of Telephoned Message

LT

ST LAZARUS VILLAGE POSTOFFICEBOX 4 ▓▓▓▓▓▓

ANYANG/SOUTHKOREA

PASSED

BILLS TODAY ▓▓▓ HOUSE OF REPRESENTATIVES SENATE NEXT STEP THANK GOD

BERNICE

MRS BERNICE GOTT▓▓LIEB
THE OUTREACH PROGRAM
BOX 1000
DOBBS FERRY NY 10522   LT/YS

Thank you for your patronage. Call again.

Telegram from Bernice to Father Lee, November 18, 1975.

A letter arrived for the Martinos at the end of December.

Dear Mr. and Mrs. Martino,

Although we are very, very far apart, we always respect and think of both of you with gratitude.

We wish all of your family a blessed new year and pray that all of your intentions may be realized.

Our two daughters are growing healthy. And they seem to think of you often. We also wish them to leave here as soon as possible, for it is a better way for them. We don't know how we can express our gratitude for your help for our children, material and spiritual, and we always find it regrettable and sorry that we cannot even write a letter to you. Really we can only say "Thank you."

How are your children? We keep your family's photo you sent me very carefully, and we show it to our children when they want to see it. Although they haven't seen you, they seem to have affection to you. We hear them speaking of "Our father and mother in America" to other children very proudly. We hear it very satisfactorily.

I will stop here with best regards.

Sincerely Yours,

Parents of your two children

Chapter 10. The Last Stretch: 1976

T hree years of hard work to turn Father Lee's and my vision into reality had put me in a state of exhaustion and insecurity. Although I felt I hadn't left a stone unturned, our bills continued to languish in the Senate and it became clear that Senator Eastland's Committee on Immigration and Naturalization did not intend to act on them in the near future, or maybe ever.

I asked Betty Edwards to accompany me on one of my lobbying efforts during those despairing days. Betty was a supportive and determined person, and I needed her to bolster whatever inner strength I still had.

We went to Washington in the first week of February 1976 and made the usual rounds in the Senate office building, talking to aides of Senator Philip Hart of Michigan, Senator John Tunney of California, Senator Hugh Scott of Pennsylvania, Senator Hiram Fong of Hawaii, and New York's Senator Javits, among others. During a meeting with Senator Fong's aide, Dorothy Parker, we got some very important information. Miss Parker told us that she had watched with empathy the machinations I had been put through on behalf of the children. She asked if I had ever contacted Edward Loughran. When I said we hadn't, she told us that in her opinion, the only way to get our stalemated bills off the shelf was to speak to him. "He is," she declared, "one of the most powerful men in this administration." Then she added, "It's almost impossible to get an appointment with him, however. But if you can somehow manage to do so, use your feminine wiles and cry—he's a sucker for a woman in tears!"

I certainly appreciated her giving me Loughran's name, but when she got to the part about crying, well, I raised my eyebrows at Betty in disapproval, out of Miss Parker's sight. We thanked her for her help and left. Once in the hallway, I shrieked, telling Betty that Miss Parker must think we were country bumpkins or something. "Use my feminine wiles and pretend to *cry!* I could never do something like that," I exclaimed righteously.

I had heard Loughran's name before in connection with Eastland's committee and I also remembered reading an article that described him as the architect for major United States immigration policy. His official title, staff director of the Subcommittee on Immigration and Naturalization, was listed in my reference book on the Congress. I made a mental note of his office location and telephone number.

Betty and I continued visiting members of the subcommittee one by one; we saw aides to Senators John McClellan of Arkansas, Ted Kennedy of Massachusetts, and Strom Thurmond of South Carolina. (The only one we couldn't seem to get to was Senator James Eastland of Mississippi; his aides always turned me down, and I could never get an appointment to see them.) Our feet ached and we removed our shoes to walk the long corridors between the Senate buildings. At each stop we repeated our plea for intervention and support. The knowledge that I should see Loughran was gnawing at me, but I was afraid to face a possible defeat and I wanted to try alternatives in case Loughran refused to see me.

It was five o'clock when we finished our rounds, and we had planned to catch the six o'clock shuttle to New York in time to join our respective families for dinner. I felt a sudden spurt of courage, however, and impetuously placed a call to Loughran's office from the lobby of his building. A woman answered, and when I asked if Mr. Loughran could see us for a few minutes, she said he had already left for the day.

"How about tomorrow?" I ventured. "It's really urgent. Please see if you can squeeze us into his schedule somehow." She hesitated and then suggested we come by at two the following day.

Betty and I were ecstatic; we couldn't believe our good fortune. "It wasn't that difficult to see him after all," Betty said. "See, I've brought you good luck." We telephoned our families in New York to tell them of our change of plans.

We arrived at one-thirty (half an hour too early) at Mr. Loughran's office the next day. As we stood outside his door, Dorothy Parker's advice came to mind and I warned Betty, in rather severe terms, that she was not to allow herself any tears in his presence; I even extracted her promise. "Otherwise," I threatened, "I will just have to see Mr. Loughran alone." I was a bundle of nerves.

I knocked timidly at his door and opened it to find a secretary at the entrance to a huge office, much bigger than those of most senators. "I'm sorry," she said, after we introduced ourselves, "but I don't have you down for an appointment today. Whom did you speak to yesterday when you called? I know it wasn't me."

"I didn't think to ask," I said.

At that moment her telephone rang and she asked the caller which hemisphere he was calling from. My nervousness increased. When she hung up, she looked at the two of us. "I am awfully sorry, Mrs. Gottlieb," she said as kindly as she could, "but Mr. Loughran has a meeting of the Judiciary Committee at two o'clock and can't possibly see you today."

My heart started thumping in my chest. I was devastated, especially after all our joyous anticipation of this moment. I quickly explained that we were from New York and had stayed overnight because of the promise by the person who answered the telephone that we would be able to see Mr. Loughran today. My voice became shaky and his secretary stared at me and Betty for a moment. Then she asked us to wait and went into Mr. Loughran's private office. She emerged a few moments later and we heard a deep voice say invitingly, "Come in, ladies."

Edward Loughran was a large and very handsome man, probably in his fifties, with piercing blue eyes, deep dimples, and bushy eyebrows. He stood up when we entered and cordially apologized for the misunderstanding. "I'm sorry I can't see you today," he said, in a nasal voice strongly resembling that of W.C. Fields. "Come in again sometime when you're visiting Washington."

I just stood there, staring at him and feeling wretchedly inadequate. I wanted to think of something clever to say that would make him change his mind, but I couldn't even form a single word. Suddenly tears came pouring down my cheeks uncontrollably. I glanced at Betty who stood frozen, an astonished look on her face.

I thanked Mr. Loughran and managed to mumble that we had exhausted ourselves for the past three years trying to get our immigration bills passed. I continued miserably, my eyes lowered, telling him that we were desperate and he was our last hope. Then I turned to the door in embarrassment.

"Just a minute," Loughran said, his voice booming across the room, and he pointed his finger at me when I turned around. "You and your idealism! You are a thorn in the side of everyone involved in immigration in Washington! What do you hope to accomplish by bringing those eight children here? Do you really think you're going to change the world?"

He *knew* who I was and what I was after! I couldn't believe it. "Yes, Mr. Loughran," I managed to say, still crying but feeling a whole lot better. "I do, and I'll tell you how. By thinking *small*, that's how!" (This inane philosophy was a product of my nervous state.)

"But that's against all we've been taught," he responded, teasing me now. "Against *everything* we've ever been taught."

He picked up his briefcase and started walking toward the door, shaking his head and muttering something to himself, but suddenly he turned around and looked at me for a long moment. I returned his stare unblinking, the tears still running down my cheeks.

"Come back in a couple of hours, "he said, an amused look crossing his face. "I'll be able to see you then."

He kept his word, and when we went back to his office around four, we ended up talking to him for almost two hours. What really surprised me was that he knew most of the details about Outreach—but he wanted to hear them from me. He just kept asking me one question after another (Betty said not a word because I'd scared her to death!). Loughran was impressed with the fact that I had done so much research. He said that when he had first heard "leprosy" or "lepers" or "Hansen's disease" mentioned in connection with our quest, he was not comfortable because it might set precedents for admitting people with other diseases.

We reviewed Outreach's whole program. He wanted to know a lot about the adoptive parents and about me—who was I, what had I studied, social work? No, I told him, I'd majored in art. He asked a million questions; he wanted to know what he was dealing with.

When he felt he had everything he needed, he stood up and walked over to a credenza piled with papers and files. He picked up a file and said, "This is your file, Mrs. Gottlieb. Where it was meant it was a file that would never be acted upon. I'm moving it here." He put it at the other end of the credenza. "These are the files that will be acted on. I want you to know, if it's the last thing I do, I'm going to see that your bills get through the 94th Congress."

After that, I saw him every time I was in Washington; we had lunch a number of times in the Senate Dining Room. If there was news from the parents in Korea or special letters, I would read him little clips; I wanted to keep him up-to-date. And I think he was genuinely interested. He'd made a decision, and he would keep his promise.

Much later, someone asked Ed Loughran if he knew me. "Do I know Bernice Gottlieb?" he said. "She's the lady who has a way of materializing through locked doors!" He also said at some point that Howard Rusk had told him, "Bernice Gottlieb is part girl and part bulldog." It sounded like an apt description to him.

Sometimes my bulldogging got no results, but sometimes it did. On February 17, one of the members of the Immigration and Naturalization Committee, Senator Hugh Scott, sent a letter to Senator Eastland about the children, which read in part:

> I understand that the immigration authorities are reluctant to allow [the children] into this country for fear of public outcry in opposition. I think this sells the American people short. These children pose no health threat to this country.

I was struck by his comment about selling the American people short. I had believed from the beginning that if people knew the facts about Hansen's disease and the children, they would have no objection whatsoever to their entering the United States. Senator Scott, at least, agreed with me!

But the years of fighting to get these children here took its toll on my family. After all, there were three children at home. Dear Fred, always so supportive, caved in a bit as well. He tried to reason with me, telling me to ask the prospective adoptive parents to take over the battle or, if my efforts continued to prove fruitless, to just give it up. This last suggestion triggered a hysterical reaction—I cried for hours from frustration, sadness, and just plain exhaustion. I realized at that point that my obsession was beyond the deep love I had for my family, and that frightened me.

Of course Fred understood what I was going through. He knew about obstacles. I was afraid to even consider the possibility of his leaving me because of the time I was investing in this quest, but I was going to keep going, even if it meant I would lose what was dearest to me by doing so. I knew it was my battle. I had started it and I had to finish it. Many lives would be negatively affected if I didn't go on, and many more would benefit if I completed my task. I felt I had no choice.

Toward the end of February, Ed Loughran told me that we had a little negotiating to do with regard to the general legislation. By this time I was really pursuing only the private bills, as these were the ones that had passed the House. The general bill was still around, but it hadn't made any progress. In the back of my mind I felt that once the eight kids were here, I could always go back and push for the general bill.

But Loughran told me that some members of Congress feared that passing the private bills would set a precedent that would lend strength to the general legislation. He said I should therefore consider asking Javits to withdraw the general bill. Otherwise Loughran felt it would become an issue (or had already become an issue) with the Senate Subcommittee on Immigration and they would hang back on passing the private bills. I couldn't let that happen.

On February 27 I wrote to Senator Javits, asking him to withdraw the general legislation so that the private bills could be passed without "setting a precedent through which the public bill [would] gain strength." I also arranged to meet with Javits's new young aide, Jeffrey Stein, who had taken over my case when Pat Shakow left. We had spoken on the phone, but this was our first personal meeting. He listened to what I had to say and immediately said it would be all right to withdraw the bill. He called Loughran while I was there and told him that a letter would be sent by messenger as soon as it was written.

Senator Eastland, the chairman of the subcommittee, wrote to Javits near the end of February to ask "what disposition you wish to be made of the bill." This may have been the first Senator Javits had heard of the plan to withdraw the bill. He threw a fit and never withdrew it; he merely asked that it be tabled. So it stays dormant but on the books, and I'm told it can be brought to life at any time. I did give Loughran a letter promising not to pursue the general bill afterwards. He took it from me and threw it in the wastebasket, saying my promise was good enough. Of course, it could be that my letter would have had no meaning if I did decide to pursue the general legislation at a later date. At any rate, Loughran's gesture made quite an impression on me at the time.

My anticipation of a meeting with Courtney Pace, the administrative aide to Senator Eastland of Mississippi, had been growing for several weeks. It was the first such meeting with a close associate of the senator, and the legendary warmth and courtly manner of this Southern gentleman had been described to me. Our bills were still being held up in Eastland's subcommittee, and I had to find a way to get them off the shelf.

I waited almost three hours past the time of my appointment, though I was the sole visitor. In the waiting room, an elderly secretary was seated at an imposing desk arranging a bunch of mimosa. She suddenly remembered me and pressed the intercom button to Mr. Pace's office. She then walked toward his door, beckoning me to follow. When she pushed his door open, I glimpsed an elderly man rising from his resting place on a couch. His pillow still bore the imprint of his head. He ran his fingers through a massive shock of white hair and straightened his clothes. I stood awkwardly at the door. His secretary made the introduction as he limped to his desk, his leg apparently having fallen asleep. He turned to face me when he reached his destination, smiled, and said, "So, yo're the lady bringing the lepers here." His southern accent was totally charming.

I gently and politely corrected him, saying the children were healthy.

"Of course, of course," he said, waving his hand to indicate he had made an error. He asked me to be seated.

"Y'know," he said, reminiscing, "a lady once came to see me with a rather terrible problem. She was anxious to become an American citizen but the authorities here were giving her an awfully hard time. Y'see, she came from a very good Jewish family who had come on bad times. It had become necessary for her to become a prostitute."

I looked at Mr. Pace, puzzled. This must be leading to something relevant, I hoped.

"When she came to see me," he continued, "she was a very desperate woman. I spent a lot of time listening to her story. I am known to be a very good judge of people's character, y'know. And as I listened to this poor woman, I believed her. I could see that she was really a very fine and cultured person who was doing what she had to do to take care of her elderly mother."

He slowly got up from his chair and paced the room, his hands clasping and unclasping behind his back. I stared out the window as he rambled on. It was not the usual elegant Washington view that one sees on television, but a rather gray-looking courtyard with an unending row of matching buildings. I wondered what he was getting at.

"Well, I decided to help this lady," Mr. Pace declared, smiling broadly. "I helped her to get her citizenship papers and I haven't been sorry. She has become a fine, respectable citizen of the United States and I am proud of her." With this last remark, he walked close to my chair and stared down at me. I returned his stare expectantly.

"Every single Christmas, she remembers to send me a lovely present. Yes, indeed, every single Christmas." He held out his hand to me. "It was so nice of you to drop by. Come see me again sometime, y'hear."

As if on cue, his secretary opened his door and I was shown out.

I had no clue what all of this meant. Obviously he was focused on the fact that I am Jewish; otherwise the story would never have come up. But even though I felt a little queasy after I left his office—I had been there for hours waiting and waiting, I had almost fallen asleep and Mr. Pace had been asleep—I felt that nothing ventured, nothing gained. I couldn't help thinking that every introduction to anybody in Washington who had anything to do with immigration was important and would eventually pay off.

When it seemed that all avenues were blocked, we had to hope and pray that the private legislation would do the trick. But Congress still had to act on the bills, and time was flying by. Weeks, then months had passed since their introduction, but nothing was moving. The 94th Congress would return from various vacation periods and not get to our legislation. I called Ed Loughran regularly every Thursday, until one week I was so depressed I didn't phone him. I was delighted when he called me and said, "Hey, how come you didn't call me today?" It was reassuring to know that he was still with the program.

A few days before Easter, I woke up before dawn, feeling really sad. Then I remembered why. The children. I thought about Senator Eastland and the Immigration Subcommittee. How could I move them? Was there something I hadn't done right? Had I thought of everything? Eastland was the stumbling block.

I tried to go back to sleep but couldn't. I quietly left the room, not to disturb Fred, passing the children's rooms to see them peacefully asleep. When I reached the library, I closed the door behind me and sat down on the couch in the dark. I could see the trees and shrubs silhouetted through the glass wall that overlooked our garden. It was usually such a pretty view, but the shadows now looked ominous.

I turned the light on and sat at the typewriter, rolling a blank sheet of paper into the machine. Like a robot, I started drafting another letter to Senator Eastland. Then I changed my mind. He must think me a crazy person by now, after all the letters I had written to him. I crumpled the paper and threw it into the basket at the side of my desk. Dear God, I thought, why don't they let the children come!

It was an ungodly hour, but I telephoned Arlene Richards in Washington. I had an idea, I told her. I asked Arlene to go to her florist and buy the largest, most obscene pot of Easter lilies she could find. She was to have it delivered to Senator Eastland with the following note stapled onto a brightly-colored ribbon:

AN EASTER PLEA TO SENATOR EASTLAND
FROM THE CHILDREN OF:
HR 1394, 1395, 1396, 1397
Suk, Hae Suk, Sang Kook, Hwa Soon, Mi Yun, Ae Sook,
Hee Kyung, Mee Kyung
Surrounded by despair and helplessness, we pray that the spirit
of Easter will fill your heart with mercy and compassion, and
through your help our years of waiting to join our parents will
finally come to an end.

Of course, I never got any response to this Easter gift, not even a note from an assistant. But I still felt that something was gained. I had to keep reminding all of them how much these bills meant to so many people.

By the end of June, nothing had happened to move the process forward. I had heard that Senator Eastland was holding up our bills because he was annoyed that his own private bills, to admit Mexican workers for his Mississippi farms, were being held up by other legislators. But there wasn't any way to make use of this information. On June 29, *The New York Times* ran a long article by Andrew H. Malcolm with the headline "Lepers and Children Count the Days."

It has been three years now since Mrs. Chin We Bum, a leper, first decided to allow her daughters to be adopted by an American family.

"Time does not heal things for us lepers," said Mrs. Chin. "I wish they could go soon. Every day hurts a little more."

The article went on to describe the children's and parents' lives in St. Lazarus and their three-year wait for the United States government to grant permission for them to come. It talked about the stigma the children faced in Korea and the hope their parents felt for their future, even in the midst of their pain at losing them. It quoted Te Chong Cho's words:

"The longer it takes, the harder it gets....Once we decide to separate, it should be fast. We can't have the idea hanging on our heads all the time....[The decision to let the children be adopted] is just one more kind of pain that comes with leprosy, but we must accept the sacrifice for their future."

"We are not normal and we know it," Mrs. Chin said, "but our children are guiltless. Why should we cling to them just for ourselves?"

"We tell the children," Mr. Cho said, "that they are going to a nice place and everything will be happiness there for them."

As he spoke, a tear rolled down his wife's cheek.

"Being a man," he added, "I am tough so, of course, nothing bothers me. But it is hard on my wife."

Nearby, Mr. Chin cleared his throat.

22   L   *family/style*   THE NEW YORK TIMES, TUESDAY, JUNE 29, 1976

Lepers and Children Count the Days

By ANDREW H. MALCOLM
Special to The New York Times

ANTANG, South Korea—

> "Once we decide
> to separate,
> it should be fast.
> We can't have
> the idea hanging
> on our heads
> all the time."

이시 앙의 우리탁 아동원 사랑의 씨를 ...

SOONER OR LATER THE SEEDS OF OUR LOVE WILL GROW

Cho Te Chong, a leper, and his wife are sending their two oldest children to a New York State family for adoption. The baby will remain at home. Right, the Rev. Alexander Lee, who helps with the adoptions.

The New York Times published several supportive articles during our years of waiting.

133

"If the girls stayed," he said, drawing lines in the dust with the toe of his shoe, "and they grew up and had boyfriends and they found that the girls' parents were lepers, then our daughters would forever have hearts stamped with pain. The future for them here is bleak. They must go. Me and my wife would like our misery to end with this generation."

Ed Mezvinsky entered the whole article in the Congressional Record on July 2.

Once again, many people responded to this new article. They sent money to support Outreach, too. One woman wrote from Massachusetts:

Dear Mrs. Gottlieb,

I read of your efforts to help the tragic situation the Korean lepers find themselves trapped in. I'm sure the enclosed cannot help much but it is sent with the greatest sympathy.

Another sent a letter from New Jersey:

Dear Ms. Gottlieb:

I just read an article about you in the New York Times concerning your work with the Korean lepers.

I know the good Lord will reward you and Father Lee for your efforts.

Please accept this small gift for Operation Outreach. Our prayers are with you.

Such donations were very welcome, and we were kept busy replying to all the expressions of encouragement and support. And meanwhile, we waited and waited.

Chapter 11. Answered Prayers

Finally, on August 5, 1976, the private bills were passed by the Senate Judiciary Committee. On August 14, the bills were approved by the Senate and signed by President Ford. To say we were all overjoyed would not begin to describe our happiness.

The telephone lines were continually busy as the adoptive parents and I called one another, laughed and cried, discussed what needed to be done, exchanged congratulations, and tried to work out details of time and place. I quickly began to make the necessary arrangements, including obtaining visas for the children. Korean Air Lines had offered to pay the children's fares, but there were many other practical matters to deal with.

I was thrilled, of course, and tremendously relieved. The stress that had gripped me since my first meeting with Father Lee was lifted, and the release was astonishing—I hadn't known how tense I was all this time. But in truth, there was a bit of letdown as well. The project that had consumed all my thoughts and actions for so long was finished.

In early September I received a lovely letter from Betty and Peter Edwards.

Dearest Bernice,

As I sit here writing to you with so much joy in my heart, I reflect back over the past three years of all that has happened to us. Of our first meeting, and of our desire to be with you all the way on the program you called Outreach. To me Outreach is an understatement, because what you have done has far Outreached anything that I could comprehend. The time you have spent, the anxieties and worry, traveling, loss of family life, because of your great desire to help your fellow man is the greatest humanitarian act that could ever be, as far as I am concerned, which at times we thought we were attempting the impossible, but your courage, comfort and your desire to win pulled us through those very trying, sad, and often despairing days....

Fred, I want to thank you too from the bottom of my heart for being the kind of person you are, for without your help, guidance and patience with us all, we surely couldn't have managed. You were our strength, because at times we were ready to do all the wrong things as you well know. But you always guided us in the right direction, for which we are truly thankful.

Bernice, you are such a wonderful person in every sense of the word....I can truly say to you, The seeds of your love have grown in our hearts. Thank you so very much for giving us our two lovely new daughters. Your family will always be a part of ours.

I arrived at St. Lazarus Village a few minutes past midnight on October 8. Father Lee took me directly to Marianna House, the new nuns' dormitory. I was shown to a pleasant room with an American-style bed reserved for foreign visitors. An inviting feather comforter was neatly turned down and a Japanese-made heater was going full blast. Cockroaches with grasshopper legs leapt about when I turned the lights on. Once settled, I parted the curtains and saw the newly built church on the high point of the mountain. Below it and to one side, the rooftops of the surrounding buildings housing the positive patients shone in the moonlight.

I was unable to sleep, only dozing off near morning. The melodic sound of bells woke me. This was followed by Father Lee chanting the mass on the loudspeaker. I heard shuffling sounds in the hall. Cold and sleepy, I got out of bed to open the door. Four nuns with shiny faces giggled when they saw me, then shyly hurried away. They had left a brass teakettle filled with steaming water and a linen-covered bowl of fresh fruit outside my door.

Day was breaking. I left the room and headed toward the church, walking across a rickety footbridge that stretched above a waterfall. Minutes before, watching the nuns depart, I had marveled at how they could cross this narrow bridge in semi-darkness, their faces buried in prayer books. The height and rushing water were intimidating.

After the service Father Lee told me the parents of the eight children were gathered in the garden near my quarters, waiting for me. Behind Marianna House, on a green knoll overlooking the fragile little bridge, was a lean-to with a thatched roof supported by four posts. It had started to rain very hard. The parents were silently huddled in the lean-to on rough-hewn benches, their faces brightening as I approached.

As soon as I joined them, they began asking questions. Would their child's American parents know what to do about her allergies? What kinds of clothes would their children need? How much clothing and other things could they take with them to America? Did they need to take money with them? Above all, would their American parents take care of these precious children? The parents were a rag-taggedy group, but their questions were those any parent would have in their situation. What they wanted most was reassurance, and I did my best to give it to them.

Bernice and Father Lee with seven of the eight children the night before leaving for America.

I left Korea on October 14, 1976, with the eight children.

Our Korean Air Lines flight was at 9:00 p.m. Kimpo airport is about fifteen miles from St. Lazarus Village and we wanted to allow at least an hour and a half, so we planned to leave the village no later than 7:30 p.m.

In the morning we pressed the clothes the children were going to wear on the plane. Martha Yoon, a highly educated and very enthusiastic member of the helpers' group that supported St. Lazarus Village, had had traditional Korean hanboks made for them as gifts. The children's parents had a last meeting with me and this time the village leader, Mr. Kwon, was present. He told me that he had been called in to solve a problem. It seemed that the parents and many of their friends from the village had planned to come to Kimpo with us, but now they had been told that Father Lee would not allow it. He thought it would be too difficult for everyone and that the scene at the airport would be too emotional. The parents asked for my intervention, as they had already hired a bus to take them to the airport and it would be a great disappointment if they could not see their children off.

My main concern, which I expressed honestly to the parents and Mr. Kwon, was that the parents' appearance at the airport might be upsetting to the children; I felt Father Lee was probably correct that making the final goodbyes at the village would be easier on everyone. However, as the parents wished to be with their children up to the very last moment, I had no choice but to agree. I went from parent to parent, holding them for long moments as they showed their appreciation.

We had our dinner early and afterwards walked uphill for a special service at the chapel where most of the village had gathered. The church was noisy, with camera crews from NBC and KBS present. The children sat in the first row, closest to the altar, dressed in their new hanboks, each with a rose pinned to it. Behind them sat their parents, holding prayer books and rosaries. It was a touching scene, interrupted only when Father Lee chastised an NBC cameraman for filming deformed patients who were praying.

The service over, hurried goodbyes were said and we rushed into four waiting cars, the eight children divided among us. It was so hectic that it took me a while to realize that the bus filled with St. Lazarus villagers was right behind us, following closely all the way to Kimpo.

Once there, with time growing shorter, we ushered the children quickly inside. The crowds were incredible and our many pieces of luggage were scattered all over the place. Upstairs, after clearing security, with little Hee Kyung clutching me tightly, I filled out a multitude of travel forms while Korean and American media representatives kept interviewing us every few moments. Some sixty patients, deformed, ragged, and on crutches, had joined the children and escorts, and crowds of curious travelers gathered to watch the strange scene.

The last goodbyes of parents and children were courageous, the parents reminding the children to behave themselves, to write, and to brush their teeth, as if they were on their way to summer camp. The children were excited and there were very few tears. I think only Mi Yun, who had been so cheerful the entire time, cried at the very last moment.

The children dressed in their hanboks with Martha Yoon, Father Lee, and Bernice at Kimpo Airport, waiting to depart for America.

From the *Korea Herald*, October 14, 1976:

Lepers' Kids Leave for U.S. Homes

First Such Adoptions

Eight healthy children, in their colorful Korean costumes, are on their way to the United States to live with their adoptive parents.

All children of former leprosy patients, they left Seoul last night aboard a Korean Air Lines (KAL) plane for Los Angeles, where they will change planes for flights to their new homes.

[After descriptions of the eight children and the adoptive parents they would go to,] The eight are enroute to a country where the adoption of healthy children is considered normal even if their parents were once leprosy patients.

"The adoption of such children in Korea would still be regarded as taboo," said Fr. Lee.

Articles like this one made me hopeful that a change in long-held ideas was beginning to happen as a result of our work.

The two littlest sisters fell asleep on either side of me right after the giant jet took off. Mee Kyung's tiny bare feet were stretched across my lap and Hee Kyung had nestled her head into my side. I didn't dare move for fear of waking them. Across the aisle, Ae Sook and Mi Yun chatted quietly, their hanboks pressed down by seat belts. The other four children sat behind us on both sides of the aisle, flanked by Father Lee and Martha Yoon. They were quiet. I couldn't tell if they were awake.

As the flight wore on, I found I was unable to sleep. Too many thoughts raced through my head. I felt an odd numbness, probably a reaction to my exhilarating high, I thought. We had left Seoul several hours earlier, bound for Los Angeles; after switching to a TWA flight, we would go on to Kennedy Airport in New York. As the children went through the customs area in Los Angeles, a burly customs agent said words to them that I have never forgotten: "Welcome to the United States. We are really proud to have you here."

We changed planes and took off for New York, and contentment engulfed me. I had my reward, heading home with the children after four long years of waiting. I had not fully realized until now that the ordeal was over. Maybe that's why I couldn't sleep? I feared awakening and finding that this wasn't really happening.

There was an announcement in Korean, followed by an English translation, both of which were unintelligible to me. Passengers craned their necks to the right, peering at something pointed out to them by the pilot. I didn't move, except to hold the children a little tighter. Nothing else mattered.

October 14, 1976, New York City.
A crush of media was waiting for us at Kennedy Airport. I felt dazed from the long flight, but never happier. I had awakened two hours before we landed and had already freshened up in anticipation of our arrival in New York. I looked around me, with deep affection, at the sleeping children in their airplane seats. They looked beautiful to me and I paused at each seat to study them. I could hardly contain myself until we landed in New York and I would share the happiness I felt with my family and the adoptive parents.

I woke two children at a time, helping them to wash and dress. I kept Hee Kyung, the smallest, for last so her cheerful chatter wouldn't disturb the sleeping passengers. Half an hour before our scheduled landing, all the children were washed, combed, and dressed in their traditional Korean clothes. Suddenly the plane dropped through the clouds and a coastline was visible. The seat belt sign went on and the children started shrieking with delight. "America, America," they screamed, like all other immigrants from time immemorial. They knew they were finally home.

TWA Security asked us to remain on the plane until all the other passengers had disembarked. It seemed forever until we heard sounds again. The adoptive parents came in first, followed by my husband and Marjorie Margolies, who was there with NBC News. They all ran toward us, unable to contain their emotion. We cried and hugged each other, one at a time for long moments. It was a deeply moving welcome.

But now we had to face the waiting press outside. There were several hundred people there, and TWA set up a press room to handle the crowd. The children were united with their respective families, completely awed by the attention they were getting. Every so often, one of them would come over to hug me or say hello and then run off again to talk to their new brothers and sisters and grandparents.

Five-year-old Mee Kyung started to cry when it came time for us to leave the airport, and she came to me to be comforted. Janet and Louis, her new parents, were anxious to start for home, but Mee Kyung clung stubbornly to me. I think that I clung to her just as much. Everyone had left, and the last TV cameramen were packing their gear. Finally Janet said, firmly but kindly, "Bernice, you're just going to have to let go of her and let me take her. She's going to have to come with us!"

It was really hard to give her up. I watched as the last of my children left the airport.

The Eight Children

Suk Chin, March 18, 1969

Hae Suk Chin, September 24, 1971

Mee Kyung Cho, January 23, 1971

Hee Kyung Cho, July 11, 1973

Sang Kook Choi, December 27, 1962

Hwa Soon Choi, December 7, 1963

Ae Sook Song, May 16, 1961

Mi Yun Lee, November 14, 1964

Chapter 12. Living in the United States

Once the children were finally here, I felt a tremendous relief and a relaxation of the tension that I'd carried with me for four years. The adoptive parents felt this as well, I believe. They and the children were occupied with getting to know one another and establishing their new family routines and relationships. There wasn't much extra time, and I think we all felt a bit burned out. In any case, I had very little contact with any of the families until April 1977, when everyone but Arlene and her two girls came to my home for a mini-reunion. None of them had seen one another since their children's arrival in October, and we had a wonderful time. Georgia Dullea, who had written about Operation Outreach in *The New York Times* in April 1974, wrote a follow-up article almost exactly three years later, on April 4, 1977.

For Korean Lepers' Children,
It's America the Beautiful

Six South Korean children, branded "untouchable" in their native country, were guests of honor at a small reunion party here.

They had not seen one another since last October when a plane carried them away from a South Korean leper colony, away from the stigma that still surrounds the healthy children of leprosy victims, to a strange land and a new life with their adopted American families.

A lot has happened since last October, so there was much party talk, most of it in English. ...

{Letting the children be adopted] was a painful decision for the parents. As Cho Te Chong, the father of Mee Kyung and Hee Kyung, told a reporter...: "It is just one more kind of pain that comes with leprosy. We must accept the sacrifice for their future."

And Mrs. Gottlieb, seeing the depth of that sacrifice, sensed that it might mean a future—not only for these few children but also for thousands of others in leprosy settlements around South Korea.

If Koreans saw that Americans accepted these children, she reasoned, they might come to accept them, too. That was the plan. And, after four years and miles of bureaucratic red tape, they're finally here, living two apiece in four different households—in Long Island, Putnam County and Washington.

The article went on to describe how well the children had settled into their new families, how much contact they had maintained with their Korean families, and how easily their new communities had accepted them.

146

Over the years after the eight children arrived, I heard from Betty and Peter from time to time and also from Janet, who had become active in the adoption movement for children with Down syndrome. But after that first gathering, we didn't get together again as a group until 2001, when we had a 25-year reunion.

The 25th reunion in 2001 at Dobbs Ferry, New York.

Excerpts from a letter to Fred and me, March 2002, from Mi Yun:

Dear Bernice and Fred,

It was really great to see you at Mee Kyung's house. Isn't it a miracle that everyone is found after such a long time has gone by? I can hardly believe it myself. ...

Everyone's faces remained the same as I remembered them when they were little tots. When we were watching the video, it touched me greatly to see Hae Suk who was unsteady at walking and how much time has gone by....

As you were pulling away from the house, we were all waving to you, and I commented to Julian that it is so amazing because all of us here are a direct result of Bernice's and Fred's efforts to bring us to the U.S. All the husbands and all the children are results of your tireless efforts and we have much to be grateful for. Thank you.

I am very happy that I was adopted because I have a wonderful life now. I am so happy that I found Ralph, my soul mate, and our three healthy children. This would not be possible without Father Lee's and your vision and all the adoptive parents who wanted to help us. I am eternally grateful to all of you. I also have to thank your children for sharing their parents with us. I am sure that four years of their lives weren't so easy for them. I am sure they missed you a lot.

It is so sad that Mr. and Mrs. Edwards aren't here anymore. I miss them a lot. They were wonderful and kind people....We loved visiting them in North Carolina and they loved Ralph as soon as they knew he was my boyfriend....

Thank you for giving all of us the chance to make our lives a better one. I believe that if I had remained in Korea, I would not have had a very good life or happy life for many reasons.

I am also grateful that I always had a very strong and close relationship with my biological family and Korean culture. They have been so wonderful to me. When I was getting my master's degree, I was struggling to pay the tuition, and my parents would send me tuition money so I could complete my studies. Education was their top priority. I always knew deep inside that they loved me and they only gave me up for adoption because they believed that I would have a better chance of leading a good and happy life, and they are right....

love, Mi Yun

P.S. Ralph felt that I should send you a copy of Hae Suk's e-mail because it is profound and touching.

March 27, 2002

Hi, Mi Yun!

I really had a great time visiting with all of you last Sunday. Talking to Bernice was great. I knew the overall "big" picture of why and how we were adopted, but never knew the details until I talked with Bernice. I find that as I get older, I am more curious about the details. I truly don't think that knowing all the details will change who I am or how I feel about myself, but it gives me a sense of understanding....

I do feel very fortunate that Suk and I were able to remain together. She and I are like one person sometimes. My adoptive mother gave us a very good, but different and disciplined upbringing. She never hid our past from us and was always open about our adoption. I think maybe that is the reason Suk and I are at peace with being adopted. I feel gratitude toward my birth mother for being strong enough to let us go when she realized she wanted us to have a better life than hers. As a mother, I know I want my son to have an even better life than mine...I try very hard and am able to provide him with the tools he needs to create a good life for himself. And I can't imagine the heartbreak my birth mother felt when she realized she wasn't able to provide Suk and me with any tools to improve our lives. So, as one mother to another, I can understand the amount of love, sacrifice, and courage it took her to give her daughters to someone she knew was able to provide her girls with the better life she wanted us to have.

You are helping me understand the kind of person I was when I was a little girl. I have very little memory of my life in Korea. I am curious about what kind of baby I was. Thank you so much for sharing your memories!...

I am getting an album together to send to Korea, to show my birth mother the wonderful life she allowed me to have. On Sunday, I saw the beautiful families we all have here in America and couldn't help but think that we are probably making our Korean parents proud by doing so well in our lives, with the opportunity they gave us.

...

Take care, Hae Suk

And a note to me from Mee Kyung:

Dear Bernice,

Enclosed are the pictures from the reunion...It was long overdue and it felt good to see everyone for the first time in 25 years!

It was reaffirming to see us happy with our families, to know that we made the best of our situations stemming from the adoptions. I consider myself very lucky that I have a wonderful life here in the U.S., full of opportunity and choices, able to have a family, without a stigma AND to still have my Korean family and a life in Korea full of connections and memories and my family's love. You have given us the best of both worlds, and I can see why my Korean parents consider you an angel!

Looking over the folder of documents you handed out to us, it's absolutely mind-boggling to read about the long struggle to get us here—it took a lot of time, effort and heartache. Thank you, Bernice; you left me a wonderful legacy to tell my son....

I think your journal/diary is a great idea. I admit, it is painful to hear of the past but it is also healing in other ways. Because I was so young, my memories are very few, so

I want to know and hear your account of how it all started. It's important to know—what you started was so special in that all the people involved (including yourself, of course) brought a lot of love and hope, trust, determination, guts, and a real humane goal to fight this awful stigma and save some children's lives and give our parents a real joy through their sacrifice...our story deserves to be told.

We had another reunion in 2006. It was hard to believe that thirty years had passed since that wonderful flight from Seoul to JFK. Sang Kook, the only boy, had returned to Korea permanently after finishing college, and his sister Hwa Soon was out of town. But all six of the others were there, and it was marvelous to see them with their children. I think they have all had good lives in the United States. Many of them have gone to Korea to see their original families, and many of their Korean family members have come here to visit; I have always been so pleased that they stayed in touch as we had promised in the beginning. I hear from some of them often, and I'm very attached to all of these brave and very special people.

I look back and think that yes, it was hard work, but we did it right. I couldn't go through it again, though—it was devastating for my own family. I'm just glad that it was successful. In the end, my family was very proud of me and what I had accomplished. I received many nice honors afterward, including the Ellis Island medal of honor in 1998, but those weren't really important. On the plane, bringing the eight children from Korea, I said, "Thank you, God, I'll never ask for anything again." And I meant it.

Articles by Sun-young Choi, staff writer at the *Korea Daily* newspaper in New York City, September, 2006

Eight Children, Who Departed from Parents with Hansen's Disease 30 Years Ago, Gather Together

"The bias and discrimination in the Korean society that has divided us from our parents should no longer exist."

Eight children who were adopted to the United States from the parents who were suffering from Hansen's disease, commonly known as leprosy, 30 years ago are having a reunion in October.

The gathering has been pushed by Mee Kyung (35) and her sister Hee Kyung (33) since 2001....

The two sisters have grown up into healthy women, only to prove the bias that Hansen's disease is hereditary was wrong. Though their life story is a delicate one to share, they decided to agree to an interview in the hope that their pain will not be repeated in Korean society.

The sisters were brought to the States in October 1976 from the Saint Lazarus Village in Anyang, Gyeonggi Province, where people with Hansen's disease lived. Unlike other adoptions, in which the background information of the children is kept hidden, the adoption of the children was rather public, especially about their leprosy parents, drawing controversy and intense media coverage.

The process of the adoption was such a big deal. Both nations had to deal with the issue for four years. The picture of the eight children holding Korean flags at the Kimpo International Airport was run in major newspapers such as the New York Times and the International Herald Tribune.

Mee Kyung and Hee Kyung, who were five and three years old back then, were fortunately adopted together by the family of a New York policeman. Growing up, the sisters depended on each other. Their new parents were also very affectionate people, Mee Kyung said.

After [more than] ten years had passed, the sisters met with their Korean parents again. Even though they kept in touch with one another through letters, cards, and tapes, with the adoptive parents' consent, it took a long time for them to meet again. "I was 21 and my sister was 19 when we met our Korean parents again," said Mee Kyung. "When we went to their house, the letters and cards we'd written in the past filled one entire wall of their room. The only joy for our parents was to hear from us. It is heartbreaking to think about the sacrifice they made for us."

"Luckily, I was the youngest among the eight at the time of the adoption. I don't even want to imagine how I would have taken it if I was older," said Hee Kyung.

Currently, Mee Kyung works at a law firm and Hee Kyung works as a manager at a hospital in Manhattan. Both said they are happily married. Still, they have unresolved pain and resentment against the bias and discrimination in Korean society....

Another adoptee among the eight...was adopted at the age of twelve, and she has an unhealed scar in the memory of the painful departure from her parents. A teacher in a New York school, she recently sent a letter.

"My father, despite his different appearance, was the kindest man I've ever known. It was such a tough experience to leave my parents at that age. It was all because I was born in a society where they saw the disease as a punishment from heaven, based on unscientific belief. Because I was adopted, I've lived a life without discrimination and became an advocate of children. I hope my pain is the last pain of children with leprosy parents. I hope the Korean society becomes kinder and warmer to the unfortunate."

"I want to let them know how well and healthy these children are"

An Interview with Ms. Bernice Gottlieb, who arranged the adoption of the eight children 30 years ago

The adoptions that brought eight children of parents with leprosy was made possible by Ms. Bernice Gottlieb, who currently lives in Dobbs Ferry, New York.

Ms. Gottlieb, who had been involved with adoption for a while, was asked for a special favor by a Catholic priest in 1972. It was a desperate suggestion to give an opportunity for a better life to children of parents with Hansen's disease, who suffered harsh discrimination in Korean society.

Ms. Gottlieb, who was already raising an adopted child from Korea, said she wanted to help these kids but didn't know much about Hansen's disease at first. So she studied. She also learned how harshly Korean society shunned the people who suffered from Hansen's disease, who were often called "Moondoonggi."

"Hansen's disease, which attacks the nerve and skin cells, is almost non-contagious and is not hereditary. But in Korea, they perceived the disease as deadly, incurable, and so contagious you can't even touch a patient." said Ms. Gottlieb.

She said she felt deep compassion for the children who couldn't escape the vicious cycle of misery just because their parents suffered a disease. The children were often called "mikama." "That's why I couldn't help but bring the children here. I couldn't give up because I thought it would send a strong message to Koreans."

Ms. Gottlieb visited Saint Lazarus Village in 1972 to meet with the parents and the children. The parents were desperate.

"Miserable life should end with our generation. Please give our children a chance for a better life," one parent said. They wanted to send their children to the States, but under one condition—that they could keep in touch with the children.

So, under the name "Operation Outreach," Ms. Gottlieb started the process of the adoptions.

The process was not simple, however. First, the relevant laws in Korea became obstacles, since they limited the age of adoptive parents and set other conditions.

But even with the Korean government's support for the adoptions, American laws got in the way. So she had to visit Washington, D.C., 42 times to lobby for revisions to the laws. Many politicians, including Jacob Javits, sponsored the bill. Finally, the children were admitted to the States.

Ms. Gottlieb clearly remembers the day when the children in hanbok, or traditional Korean costume, said goodbye to their parents. It was an emotional day. Tears ran down the faces of people who were sending their treasure and only source of joy to the other side of the world. They asked, "Will our children be well fed and happy? They won't be slaves or maids, right?"

Ms. Gottlieb said she is so proud that the children blossomed into happy and healthy adults. "I want all Koreans to see how well and happy these children are. I hope there is no more bias against people with Hansen's disease. And no more 'moondoonggi' and no more 'mikama.'"

And this is Mi Yun's letter to the reporter who wrote these two articles:

September 22, 2006
Dear Sun Young,

...I never expected to write about my childhood, but in the light of recent talks with Bernice, I would like to contribute my reflection of my personal journey.

I can only give you a short summary of my experience, but it should shed some light onto the very complex issues that surround adoption. As we agreed, you will not use my name...I want my identity kept private.

Through the child's eyes

What do children know when they are so young? I was told that the streets of America are paved in gold. The grown-ups in Korea told me that I would be forever happy because I would never suffer and I would be well taken care of because Americans are so rich. Perhaps the grown-ups felt sorry for me and they had to make up these tall tales, or perhaps they truly believed that America was this way. I am not angry with them because they were trying to make me feel less frightened. Perhaps the grown-ups saw a way out for me from the future discrimination that I would experience because I was a child of parents with leprosy. Through the child's eyes, she was only trying to please her parents by accepting her fate.

Leprosy is also known as Hansen's disease, and it caused my father to have disfigurement in his hands and feet and also a small bit on his face; specifically, his nose was sunken because the cartilages had deteriorated. Many of the villagers had these physical disfigurements resulting from not receiving the proper medicine soon enough. But through the child's eyes, the child could only accept them as normal because the child was taught not to notice and to accept everyone as equal. Through the child's eyes, the child only saw who they were, kind human beings no matter what they looked like. I remember my father struggling to bandage his wounded foot, using his mouth to hold the bandage because of his unusable hands. Seeing this struggle, his daughter jumped right in and helped him finish bandaging his stubborn deep open wound that would not heal for many years. It made her feel good to be useful to him, because she loved him. Through the child's eyes, she loved him and would do anything to make his life better.

You have to ask yourself what kind of desperate situation would lead a mother to give up her child to strangers who lived so many thousands of miles away, with the possibility of never seeing her daughter again. The mother's heartache of believing she had made a terrible mistake. The mother's anguish and guilt, thinking she is a terrible mother and wishing that she could undo what she had done. The father's loss of his first-born and the only person who was so compassionate to him in his sufferings. The brother, too young to fully grasp this huge spectrum of sadness but knowing something is very wrong. But do not fear, mother, I am not mad at you. You must have felt such despair that you wanted me to escape my future of being shunned in an intolerant Korean society which still exists, and all because I was a child of parents with Hansen's disease. When you read this article, mother, do not shed any more tears, because your daughter has become a fully evolved woman without prejudice. I have become a child's advocate. I have become an educator, and I can help my students to become kind, compassionate and respectful people. I am a product of the loving St. Lazarus Village.

I loved living with my family in Korea. I often reminisce about my small quaint village and all the people in it. In this small village, everybody cared about each other. We all had a common thread between us. Most of the adults who lived in this village had Hansen's disease. In my eyes, I did not notice their disfigurements; instead, I saw them as Ajuma and Ajuhsee [honorary aunt and uncle]. I would always bow happily to all the elders in the village. The formality made me feel some sense of duty and I knew where I stood in the hierarchy of my village. Every single person who lived in this village treated everyone else with respect and was generally very kind. Of course, as with any cross-section of population, there were good things and bad things in the village, because we are all humans. There was domestic violence and alcoholism in the village. My adopted father once told me that perhaps alcohol helped ease the intolerable pain they felt because their family and society had abandoned and shunned them.

My father seldom went outside the village because Korean people would treat him badly and look at him with disgust. Shame on you! You did not even know what a wonderful man he was.

I have blocked out the day I left Kimpo airport in 1976. All I can remember was being very, very scared. I thought I would never see my parents, my younger brother, my friends, and all the villagers again. That day we all died a little. I kept reciting my mother's name, my father's name, and my brother's name, and telling myself never to forget them. I was so afraid that I would forget them and that I would never see them again. My heart broke into a million pieces. I clung to the meager possessions I had brought with me on the airplane and I kept staring at them as if those objects would somehow comfort me and reassure me. What does a child know about the world? Not much. It was a very, very sad day.

Now I am a mature woman and I see my sad departure as a direct result of Korean society's attitude toward leprosy victims. Leprosy was an ugly word to a lots of Korean people. They were misled and misinformed by unrealistic fears that were not based on the scientific facts about the disease and the difficulty of actually catching it. Korean society treated leprosy victims like subhumans not worthy of common human dignity. This fearful and judgmental Korean society stripped my people of any self-worth. Perhaps now you can understand how a mother could have done the unthinkable, surrendering her daughter in hopes that the child would have a better life without any discrimination.

My American parents were very kind. They adopted five Korean children, two from the village. They have now passed on, but they tried their best to provide all of us with a proper upbringing. My adopted parents took one of my adopted sisters and me back to see our parents in 1979. It is amazing that they took us back to our biological parents; they wanted us to have a close relationship with them. I owe tremendous gratitude to my American parents for reuniting me with my biological family. Of course, as with any family, there were problems in this household. However, I am grateful that they had room to help one more child.

. . .

Bernice Gottlieb and her family are incredibly caring and giving people. Bernice saw a vision of freeing us from our desperate situation of ill treatment from our own countrymen, and she was able to give us a brighter future through her hard work and sacrifice. I am thankful that Bernice took up our cause, because it gave me a chance to become a more reflective and profound thinker and to help other people in the future.

I hope this unique story will inspire others to become more sensitive to some people's misfortune and not ostracize them. We are all the same. We breathe the same air and want the same things in life, and everyone of us deserves to be treated with respect, no matter what our condition. Furthermore, all of us want to find the balance of living our lives productively in hopes of finding our happiness. One cannot be so narrow-minded and become blind to compassion. One has to seek for a higher purpose in life and contribute to your fellow men and teach the value of kindness. Our hope for the future is how we educate our children. One cannot teach hate. One has to become respectful of all kinds of people.

Afterword

Late in 1975, I was invited by the Indian Red Cross and the Hind Kusht Nivaran Sangh (Indian Leprosy Association) to visit India; HKNS was the central clearing house for leprosy projects in India, and the purpose of my visit was to see how Outreach might help improve the quality of life for children of leprosy patients there. My visit was for a little more than three weeks in January 1976. HKNS planned a complete itinerary for me, which included a week in New Delhi and then shorter visits to Madras, Bombay and surrounding areas of these major centers.

In Delhi I met a lot of people connected with private welfare organizations and government programs; I visited leprosy colonies, leprosy homes, orphanages, and children's homes. I talked with people who were in charge of the public information campaign to wipe out myths about leprosy, which was credited with making it possible for the children of leprosy patients to attend public schools, in contrast with Korea. And I saw research centers where important work on drugs was being conducted. Though far from perfect, the situation in Delhi seemed to be moving in positive directions.

In Madras I saw the work being done by the German Leprosy Association, run by both Indians and Germans. Free treatment in outpatient clinics was offered to patients, and special sandals made from old automobile tires were sold to the patients at a very low price (having to pay a few paisas helped prevent the patients from losing the shoes and coming back in a few days for another pair). They were also carrying out a screening program in schools, where they found that 13 of every 1,000 children examined were infected with leprosy. And they had set up a program to lend small amounts of money to patients to allow them to start businesses (a precursor of today's micro-lending programs).

In Bombay the situation was worse than what I had seen elsewhere. There were many more orphanages; I saw children in a women's prison with their sick mothers; I visited leprosy villages where no work was available and patients and ex-patients lived in dung-covered huts with straw roofs or in hutments on the streets nearby. Outside the city, I saw women washing their clothes and cooking with water from Bombay's sewers—the only water available to them. Their children in the huts were burning up with fever from malaria and cholera and dying from complications of measles. These sights were pitiful and unforgettable. Clean water is a universal problem in the third world.

India was beautiful in so many ways, but its poverty was evident everywhere. One experience was emblematic. When I arrived in Madras, I was met at the airport by Drs. Gershon and Mani. They asked where I was staying and were quite shocked when I told them I was going to the Intercontinental Hotel. "It's so expensive," they said, "why don't you stay at an Indian hotel, which would be much cheaper?" I thought, Why not?, so they took me to the Gupta Hotel. When they dropped me off, they said they would be back to pick me up for dinner at five p.m.

At a leprosy village near Bombay, Bernice took some of the
children to a shop for ice cream and sweet treats.

I had gotten up very early for the flight, I was exhausted and hot,
and all I could think about was a shower and a nap. But when I got to
my room, I saw a sign in the bathroom—there would be no water until
seven p.m. All right, I thought, I can do without a shower. The toilet
was a hole in the floor, like many others I'd seen in India, but I prided
myself on not requiring American-style luxury. The room was quite hot
and stuffy, so I found the switch and started the fan. But immediately
a cloud of mosquitoes swarmed up from the top of the fan, so I quickly
shut it off again. This was malaria country, after all. I took off my outer
clothes, thinking I would just lie down for the nap I'd been so looking
forward to. I pulled back the coverlet—and saw bedbugs. So I put my
clothes back on and went out to the Intercontinental Hotel, where I
had lunch and took a tour of Madras. At five o'clock, I went to meet the
doctors. When they heard my story, Dr. Gershon insisted that I come
and stay at his home above the city, so all ended well. But it showed

me an India that cost far more than most Indians could pay but was so much poorer than what we are used to in the United States.

My visit to India led me to conclude that Outreach should have a different thrust in India from its purpose in Korea. I saw that the children of leprosy patients were integrated into Indian society if they had money for their education. Without this money, they could not afford schoolbooks (required for entering school) or proper clothes and medical examinations, also requirements. If they didn't go to school, they were sent to work, and I saw many children with occupational diseases resulting from hard labor. I therefore chose 25 children in the Bombay area to send to school under Outreach's auspices. In 1976, for $5.00 a month, we could send a child to school, buy his books and school supplies, give him medical attention and preventive care, and supply nutritional assistance if needed; for 25 children, we would need $125.00 a month. I also decided that Outreach would support the government's educational campaign about leprosy.

I felt that our adoption program in India for children of leprosy patients was less important than our school support for them; in fact, the orphans I saw were in worse straits than the children of leprosy patients and more in need of a program for adoption abroad. But after the eight Outreach children finally arrived in 1976, I had promised myself, and my family, that I would not get personally involved in trying to bring more children from other countries to the United States. As I wrote to one of my Washington contacts, "It has been much too difficult for all parties concerned and we need to find other ways to effect social change."

Meanwhile, I had begun working, under a grant from the International Federation of Anti-Leprosy Associations (ILEP) and the International Leprosy Association, on a two-year study project to evaluate the situation of children who were suffering both spiritually and physically from leprosy around the world. The study was in conjunction with the United Nations' International Year of the Child

1979 (IYC); the research focused on stigmatized children, and its goal was to understand and change social attitudes. In August 1977, ILEP sent a questionnaire to experts on leprosy around the world; it asked how many children were being treated for Hansen's disease, what the most pressing needs were (medical, surgical, financial, educational, etc.), what kinds of social injustices were suffered by children with a "leprosy background," and what stigmatizing terminology was used for such children. The cover letter for the questionnaire explained that I had been appointed an expert for this study group, a member of a special committee for coordination of activities worldwide, and liaison between ILEP and UNICEF.

Dr. Oliver Hasselblad was no longer the head of American Leprosy Missions (ALM). His position was now held by the Reverend Roger Ackley, whose views were quite different from Dr. Hasselblad's. In fact, Reverend Ackley supported my work with Outreach, and he and his associate Robert Bradburn were the ones who had invited me to work with them on the IYC leprosy project. I would report to ALM by phone or in writing twice a month and submit written reports twice a year. I was delighted, and I thought this change in attitude was both welcome and quite ironic.

My agreement with ALM said, "The purpose of this relationship is to provide assistance in bringing before the world a fuller awareness of the all-encompassing need of those children around the world who suffer, spiritually and physically, from the disease of leprosy." I was very proud to represent such a distinguished international federation of non-government organizations and even prouder of what we accomplished. One milestone was the resolution on human rights of leprosy children, which was adopted at ILEP's general assembly in November 1978. It was sent to international bodies like WHO and UNESCO and also to governments and voluntary agencies that worked with people with Hansen's disease, and it formed one of the bases for the work under ILEP's auspices. The resolution said:

Every child with leprosy, and every child coming from a
family with one or more members who have leprosy should
have the same general rights as other children, including
the right

1. to normal family life in his own community;
2. to adequate nutrition;
3. to free education in company with his contemporaries;
4. to the same opportunities for play and recreation as
   other children;
5. to appropriate medical care in general or specialized
   health facilities;
6. to special care if handicapped with discrimination
   because of leprosy.

Almost one million children were examined for leprosy during
the Year of the Child as a result of our work. I became the chairperson
of the Sub-group on Stigmatized Children of the Working Group on
the Handicapped Child of the Non-Governmental Organizations
Committee for the International Year of the Child, 1979, and I was
responsible for compiling and writing a discussion paper called "The
Fact of Stigma"; it described many different types of stigmatizing
conditions and was distributed to 140 countries. Margaret Mead's
foreword to the paper said in part:

No society that we know of cares well for all its children, nor
does any society have a monopoly of ways in which children
can be especially cherished. In discussing stigmatization, it
is important to keep in mind these two considerations....
The International Year of the Child, participated in by
the peoples of the planet, gives a chance to bring together
information about ways in which each country has special

defects to correct and special gracious customs to commend to the peoples of other nations.

I believe that this focus on stigma was a benefit that came in part from Outreach's success in bringing the eight children to America and in making their story known to so many ordinary people as well as experts.

It was a fascinating and exciting undertaking, and in the course of it I met and corresponded with many people who had considerable influence in movements for social justice and equality. First Lady Rosalynn Carter said in a December 1977 telegram, referring to the UNICEF conference, "I was most encouraged to learn about your efforts to address the very critical problem of 'stigmatized children.' It is so important that this issue receive serious attention, for the effects of stigmatization cause immeasurable damage to one of the world's most precious resources. I look forward to hearing about the results of your conference."

In July 1978, I wrote to President Park Chung Hee of South Korea in my capacity as representative to UNICEF of the two international anti-leprosy groups, ILEP and the International Leprosy Association. After commending South Korea's proposed new law that would increase educational opportunities for preschool children and adults, I reminded him of the continued segregation of children whose parents were Hansen's disease patients, and I concluded:

> Mr. President, I ask that in the final drafting of the new educational legislation, these children be given consideration for their future lives. A bill which includes the right of these children to attend normal community schools, followed by a public education program to assist their assimilation, would set a precedent in your country, inspiring other nations to follow.

The United Nations has declared 1979 to be the "International Year of the Child," and recently one very involved in this year's observance, visited Carville. Bernice Gottlieb, Chairperson of the United Nations' Working Group on Stigmatized Children and ILEP's (International Federation of Anti-Leprosy Associations) official representative to the UN ing Seminar at Carville, Gottlieb began her fight and explains that it took four separate Acts of Congress and continued support from various legislators to make the placement of the Korean children into American homes a reality. "There was no trouble finding families and many people do go overseas to seek children simply because American

Bernice Gottlieb

United Nations Names '79 Year of the Child

during this year, recently presented to members of ILEP's 20th Working Session held at Carville, a paper entitled, "The Fact of Stigma." It deals with "Stigma and Leprosy," a subject which has come under much discussion recently with regard to Hansen's disease control programs, as it relates to measured success, especially in the developing nations where the disease is most endemic. As more attention is drawn to this topic, its study continues to become a more integral part of Hansen's disease control programs.

Gottlieb became involved in HD work through her professional experience as a volunteer placing disabled children into adoptive homes. She cites her 4-year struggle to place eight perfectly healthy Korean children of "leprosy" patients into adoptive homes here in the States as her real initiation to HD. Having attended the American Leprosy Missions 1973 Spring Train-

children are less readily available." For the Korean parents, who asked Gottlieb to find the American families, this was of course the "ultimate sacrifice," but they knew their childrens' future in a stigmatized society was not a bright one. "What makes our program unique," she points out, " is that the children have continued to communicate with their Korean families through letters, tapes and photographs. Actually, they now have two families and have adjusted quite well."

As for her work at the UN this year, Gottlieb chairs one of the first working groups to be formed in observance of the International Year of the Child, one of about a dozen groups hopeful to be functioning throughout the year; "Rights of the Child," "Education of the Child," "Handicapped Children," etc. "Our goal," she explains,"is to identify groups of children who are stigmatized, bringing together

those who are interested in stigmata from diverse fields, because we believe that there are common threads in human behavior towards stigmatizing conditions."

After months of research Gottlieb's report revealed some interesting factors contributing to the perpetuation of stigmata. The following is a brief excerpt.

PARENTS We are convinced that the first and often most important stigmatization of children comes from their parents. Major efforts should be made to help parents become sensitive to the needs of their children and to understand their own emotions and insecurities with regard to stigma. Parents can learn to teach their children a positive self regard and high esteem. These strengths provide an armor and are assets that change the attitudes of others towards the child.

Marty Petty

Bernice was interviewed by the *Star*, Carville's in-house newspaper, in 1979.

Such a humane act would be the greatest contribution the Republic of Korea could make to the International Year of the Child.

Three weeks later, I received a reply from Chan Hyun Pak, Korea's minister of education:

...According to the current Education System of our nation, it makes a rule not to separate these children from their contemporaries. Therefore, with primary school pupils, they are included in general education, not in name but in reality, in case they can commute to schools in their neighborhood, while, if the schools are far away from their residence, separate schools or branch schools admit them. Moreover, these children who enter junior high schools and upper schools completely join their contemporaries in general education with no mark.

...

Let me advise you that it is hardly necessary to take legal action for the admission of these children to normal community schools because of their circumstances from their parents and the law is faithfully carried into effect. Nevertheless, we will continue to give our careful consideration on their behalf.

It was hard to know what to make of this letter. On the one hand, we knew that children from the leprosy resettlement villages did not in fact receive the same education opportunities as their contemporaries; on the other hand, Mr. Chan clearly realized that they should be given equal access to education without stigmatization. At least we had put him on notice that the world was watching.

This four-year experience was wonderful in so many ways. It felt good to know that I had contributed to such an important worldwide effort on behalf of children everywhere, and my own knowledge had been dramatically expanded as I became aware of the many other conditions besides leprosy that created stigmatization for children. I am grateful for the opportunity to have been a part of this important work, which is still ongoing almost 35 years later.

Lightning Source UK Ltd.
Milton Keynes UK
27 January 2011

166474UK00001B/147/P